straight to hell

straight to hell
20th century suicides

Namida King (editor)
ISBN 1-84068-090-3
Published 2004 by Creation Books
www.creationbooks.com

Contents

1. **Budd Dwyer** by David Kerekes & David Slater   5
2. **Pierre Molinier** by Stephen Barber   9
3. **David Rappaport** by Mikita Brottman   13
4. **Michael Ryan** by Mikita Brottman   17
5. **Adolf Hitler** by Nikolas Schreck   21
6. **Guy Debord** by Angus Carlyle   29
7. **Harry Crosby** by Jack Sargeant   37
8. **John McCollum** by Mikita Brottman   43
9. **Jim Jones** by Simon Dwyer   49
10. **Kurt Cobain** by Mikita Brottman   59
11. **Rudolf Schwarzkogler** by Stephen Barber   65
12. **Gilles Deleuze** by Julian Weaver   69
13. **Fred West** by Mikita Brottman   77
14. **Unica Zürn** by Peter Webb   83
15. **Diane Linkletter** by Mikita Brottman   97
16. **Yukio Mishima** by Stephen Barber   103
17. **David Koresh** by Mikita Brottman   107
18. **Donald Cammell** by Nikolas Schreck   111
19. **Hart Crane** by Jeremy Reed   119
20. **Heaven's Gate** by Zeena Schreck   129
21. **Mark Rothko** by Peter Whitehead   137
22. **Thomas Hamilton** by Peter Sotos   145
23. **Sid Vicious** by Alan Parker   159

budd dwyer

On 22 January 1987, R. Budd Dwyer, the Pennsylvanian State Treasurer, gave a press conference following his conviction for bribery the previous month. During his trial at the Federal District Court, officials from a Californian computer company testified that Dwyer had illegally received $300,000 to secure a lucrative contract for the company. Dwyer, 47, faced a possible 55-years in prison and was to be sentenced the following day.

Reporters believed they had been summoned to the conference to witness a resignation, but the portly man had other, more devastating intentions. Dwyer's protestations of innocence lasted almost half-an-hour, during which he claimed to be the victim of an "American Gulag". He rounded off his monologue by handing out sealed envelopes to three of his former colleagues.[1] This done, he reached for a manila envelope lying beneath documents on a desk and removed a .357 Magnum. There was a brief moment before colleagues and reporters became aware of the weapon. Then panic. Camera shutters fired rapidly as Dwyer backed to the wall warding off potential interference. "Please leave the room if this will affect you," he nonchalantly warned. The panic-stricken journalists called out, "Don't Budd... don't do it." Dwyer looked nervously from left to right and told any over-enthusiastic saviours, "This is loa... may hurt someone." And hurt somebody it did.

Gripping the barrel with his left hand, right hand on the butt and trigger, he thrust the weapon into his mouth. Before anyone could intervene, his forefinger increased the pressure on the trigger and the hammer struck the primer cap of the chambered shell. The nitro-cellulose propellant ignited in the cartridge case driving the bullet along the barrel. Super-heated discharge gasses erupted from the muzzle and vaporised the soft tissues forming the roof of Dwyer's mouth. The copper-jacketed bullet punched through the palate bone forcing a destructive path through the nasal fossa. Now deformed in shape, it travelled through Dwyer's cranial cavity at an angle of approximately 85°, propelling fragments of bone into the cerebellum, yielding excessive brain tissue destruction. The bullet struck the inner wall of his skullcap, and exited his head leaving a surprisingly neat circular hole about four-centimetres in diameter.

So rapid was the event that several cameras, whose shutter-release buttons were pressed as Dwyer pulled the trigger, caught only the falling form. With his body slumped behind the desk, television camera operators and newspaper photographers moved in. The final image of the man showed his glazed eyes slowly closing to slits, head sinking to his shoulders, and virtually his entire blood supply haemorrhaging from his nostrils. Rather optimistically, someone over the moans of the stunned onlookers could be heard to request a doctor.

At least two television cameras were present at Dwyer's press conference. The most frequently seen footage is that taken by the camera nearest to Dwyer, viewing him from his right-hand side, relatively unobscured even after he slumps to the floor. The second camera is positioned in the centre of the room, looking directly at the desk and Dwyer standing behind it. From this angle, when Dwyer falls to the floor only his head remains in shot. It is in this latter footage, following an initial glimpse of the State Treasurer as he lies bleeding, that the camera pulls away and focuses up at the wall (out of respect or possibly looking for blood splashes or brain matter). As an aide urges everyone to remain calm, the camera returns to Dwyer and the figure which now tries to veil him from the rest of the room. "You've got your footage," says the aide. "Would you kindly wrap up your footage. Get your cameras out. Please, get out of the room." The camera remains steadfast. "You've got everything that can be gotten at this point."

The aide looks to the body behind him and, voice shaking, mutters, "Oh my God in Heaven." Composing himself, he continues, "Please, that's enough. That's enough." The camera shuts off.

Dwyer was officially pronounced dead at 11.31 AM. By lunchtime his suicide was broadcast into household USA. Television station WPVI-TV in Philadelphia showed the suicide in full, as did WPXI-TV in Pittsburgh. Officials validated their decision to screen the shocking footage by calling it an "historic event". It was run again in a later broadcast but in an edited form. Several stations showed only the gun being taken from the envelope, and others cut away as Dwyer inserted the weapon into his mouth. CBS and ABC networks abstained from transmitting the videotape footage altogether and opted for a still photograph of Dwyer instead.

Later that same day, a series of photographs showing the event in sequence – the gun in Dwyer's hand, then in his mouth, and finally his head thrown back from the blast – was placed on an international transmission network preceded by a warning as to their disturbing quality. Less than 24 hours after his death, newspapers around the world gave everyone everywhere the opportunity to study Dwyer's last seconds of life. As with the television networks, the press employed their own standards of discretion in illustrating the story. All but the tabloids refrained from using the explicit photographs. "MAN SHOOTS HIMSELF ON TV" declared the front page of the *Daily Mirror*. A two-page, stage-by-stage photo-spread publicised the event, concluding on an optimum shot of Dwyer's head being shattered by the exiting bullet.[2]

1. The envelopes contained Dwyer's organ donor card, instructions for funeral arrangements, and a letter addressed to Governor Casey stating that he had not resigned his post but remained Treasurer until the end. The letter also suggested his wife should be considered as his successor.

2. Footage of Dwyer's bloody demise has featured in a slew of "shocumentary" films, including *Mondo Cane VI*, *Cathode Fuck*, *Assault Video*, *TV Disasters*, *News Nightmares*, and *Traces Of Death*. It is also known to have found its way onto the extreme music circuit and used as back projection for some bands during live performances.

First published in *Killing For Culture* (Creation Books, 1994)

pierre molinier

The French photographer and painter Pierre Molinier produced the most hallucinatory and sexually-saturated images created during the twentieth century. Revered by the Surrealists' leader André Breton but reviled by the staid inhabitants of Bordeaux, where he lived for most of his life, Molinier undertook his paintings and photographs of multiple sex acts executed by gorgeous young men and women (usually modelled by a made-up Molinier himself), using intricate superimpositions to create his imageries of multiple penetrations and fellations. Throughout his life, Molinier was obsessed with imagining and visualizing his own death – which he always envisaged as arriving through his own intervention, via a meticulously prepared act of suicide – and from 1950, he made paintings and photographs that ecstatically prefigured that terminal outrage. His father too had committed suicide and Molinier decided that it would be his own decision – not that of any deity – which would ensure his intentional exit from life.

      Molinier was born in 1900 in the southern French town of Agen, but moved to the glowering, rain-sodden Atlantic port-city of Bordeaux, with its ill-mixed population of drink-crazed sailors, prostitutes and bourgeois merchants, in 1931. He had begun photographing young women from an early age; in 1918, his young sister Julienne died, and Molinier seized the opportunity to rape her corpse after being left alone to photograph her: 'Even dead, she was beautiful. I shot sperm on her stomach and legs, and onto the First Communion dress she was wearing. She took with her into death the best of me.' The prostitutes of Bordeaux were renowned throughout France for their sheer readiness to engage in whatever acts of sexual degradation or cruelty were demanded of them, and Molinier would make full use of their proximity. He moved into a large studio at 7 rue des Faussets, a narrow alleyway in the ancient Saint Pierre district that heaved throughout the day and night with floods of whores, whistling pimps and vomiting clients. From the 1950s onwards, Molinier focused on sex as the sole subject matter of his work, interspersing it with whoring, pistol-practice and drinking. He declared: 'My mission on this earth is to transform the world into an immense brothel.' He occasionally found himself in the Bordeaux jail after taking pistol shots at his enemies and at members of his family, whom he detested. Isolated in Bordeaux, he contacted André Breton in 1952, declaring himself to be a 'pariah' who had, for decades, been working alone with the obsessions of his art; Breton immediately welcomed him into the Surrealist movement and praised him as 'the master of vertigo', although Molinier would never move permanently to Paris and his anti-religious rages and tirades would eventually become too much even for Breton. Molinier's two great projects of the 1950s were to commit incest with one of his daughters, whom he set up as the owner of a brothel, and to invent a machine which would allow him to fellate himself – after two years of assiduous work and technical experimentation, Molinier finally succeeded, and photographed himself engaged in an eighteen-day bout of self-fellatio, during which he survived on nothing but his own semen. But Molinier's third great project – to perform a testicle transplant on himself when his decades of sustained, out-and-out whoring started to put a strain on his own testicles – failed to come to fruition. However, he succeeded in devising numerous ways in which to photograph himself during acts of self-sodomy.

During the early 1970s, Molinier entered the most productive phase of his work – with his growing international notoriety, he found himself besieged by young men and women, often fifty years younger than him, determined both to be rigorously sodomized by him and to appear as models in his series of photographs, which were seen in the context of that time as a form of deviant performance art, allied to the preoccupations of such art movements as the Vienna Action Group. In 1970, on a visit to Munich, Molinier encountered the prominent Vienna Action Group artist Hermann Nitsch, and took many photographs of one of his blood-drenched performance actions of human and animal crucifixion; a young woman associated with the Vienna Action Group, who participated in Nitsch's actions as a 'model', Hanel Koeck, became Molinier's most intensive sexual and creative obsession in the first half of the 1970s, often visiting him in Bordeaux, although Molinier would also form attachments to androgynous young male artists, such as Luciano Castelli (later renowned as one of the 'Young Wild Ones' of 1980s Berlin art) and Thierry Agullo, in his final years. In all of Molinier's photographs, he himself appears as a participant, naked apart from black stockings and high-heeled shoes, at the heart of the multi-layered and multi-superimposed acts of penetration, his face masked with a permanent sneer of ecstasy.

In the mid-1970s, Molinier's health collapsed – he developed gall bladder problems and prostate cancer, for which his doctors recommended surgery that would involve the summary excision of his anus. After so many decades of relentless copulation and sodomy, Molinier noted in despair that he could no longer maintain an erection for more than several hours at a time. The moment had come for him to make his long-prepared exit. He said farewell to the generations of prostitutes in the rue des Faussets whose cunts and anuses he had diligently inhabited for so many decades.

On 3 March 1976, at the age of seventy-five, Molinier shot himself in the mouth on his bed in the rue des Faussets, having masturbated so that the terminal torrent of semen spurting

straight to hell

from his well-worn penis coincided exactly with the white-hot flash of his exploded cerebral matter. His friends were aware of his intention to commit suicide on that day, and he had arranged with them that he would send his studio cat down to the bar on the opposite side of the rue des Faussets as a signal that he was just about to blow his brains out. They arrived to find a note attached to the door of his studio: 'Being alive now makes me shit so I AM KILLING MYSELF OF MY OWN FREE WILL and I am going to have a great time doing it.' Inside, Molinier was lying on the bed, having shot a pistol-wound cleanly up through his cranium into the wall. His body, according to his intentions, was donated to medical science and the grotesquely dilapidated penis and anus of the artist were examined with horror and then dissected by young medical students. In subsequent decades, even the dour inhabitants and authorities of Bordeaux recognised that he was the only artist of significance ever to have emerged from the city, and his studio in the rue des Faussets is now marked with a plaque.

david rappaport

All dwarves may start small, but some, such as Verne Troyer and Gary Coleman, go on to make a big name for themselves in the movie business. Unfortunately, David Rappaport wasn't so lucky.

In Europe, Rappaport was probably best known for his role as Randall, leader of a band of time-travelling midgets in Terry Gilliam's *Time Bandits*. Americans, however, will mainly recall his starring role as a jovial toymaker in the hit television series "The Wizard," which aired on CBS between September 1986 and March 1987. Rappaport also appeared in twelve other movies, including *The Secret Policeman's Ball* (1980), *Sword Of The Valiant* (1983), and *Peter Gunn* (1989).

David Rappaport was born in London in November 1951 to parents of average height. As a baby, he was diagnosed with achondroplasia, a form of dwarfism that allows the trunk to grow while stunting the arms and legs. "It never stopped me from doing anything," said Rappaport in an interview with *People* magazine four years before his suicide. "I suppose if I'd wanted to play football, it would have got in the way. But it's never been a problem."

Or so he claimed.

At an early age, Rappaport displayed musical talent, learning to play the accordion and the drums. At the age of eight he began playing music to the inhabitants of nursing homes, and on one occasion was shocked to meet several dwarfs like himself. "There was nothing wrong with them," said Rappaport. "They weren't ill. They were just there because they were little. It had a chilling effect on me. I've never forgotten it." He continued to play the drums semiprofessionally at university in Bristol, where he was studying psychology. During this time he also got his first taste of the theatre, acting in a student comedy revue that eventually played professionally in London.

In 1975 he married his college girlfriend Jane, who was of conventional height and worked as a midwife; a year later she gave birth to their son, Joe, also of average height. In 1977, after working briefly as a schoolteacher, Rappaport gave up his job to devote himself full-time to a theatrical career. "It was the worst possible time to become an actor," he said. "I had a wife and a kid. But it seemed now or never, so I went with it." His first important role was in the stage production of *Illuminatus!*, a 5-part, 8-hour psychedelic science-fiction rock-opera based on the books by Robert Anton Wilson and Robert Shea.

Rappaport next moved to London, where he lived for some time in the squatted housing complexes on Freston Road in Notting Dale, whose 120 inhabitants declared themselves independent from the United Kingdom in October 1977 when they were threatened with eviction. They called this new nation-state "Frestonia," and drew the attention of the international press. The community of Frestonia was eventually rebuilt with millions of pounds of "foreign aid" to the U.K. Rappaport, who'd already appeared on children's television shows like "Tiswas" and "Jigsaw," was named Foreign Minister of Fredonia, and used the opportunity to raise his public profile by holding forth to the foreign press who flocked to the squat after its declaration of independence. He had the professional cheek to charge fifty pounds for each interview, and had a popular circus-style act which the smoking of heroic amounts of cannabis followed by a spot of blindfold knife-throwing.

Rappaport and his family moved to the U.S. after the success of 1981's *Time Bandits*, when he was approached about playing R2D2 in the original *Star Wars*. Rappaport refused, not wanting to take the role of a robot, but was soon offered more promising roles in films like 1985's *The Bride,* starring Sting and Jennifer Beals. His performance in *The Bride* led him to become increasingly popular in the U.S.; he was often invited to appear on talk shows and in guest spots, and was eventually offered the leading role on "The Wizard," widely promoted as "the first TV show in history to star a dwarf." Although the show won mixed reviews, Rappaport's performance was singled out as an unqualified success.

With his proceeds from "The Wizard," Rappaport could finally afford to lead a celebrity lifestyle. He and Jane were divorced in December 1985, and David bought himself a VW Rabbit equipped with special extended pedals and elevated seats. He started to be spotted at hot nightclubs in L.A. where he'd hang out with friends like Sting, Trudie Styler and Rosanna Arquette.

But "The Wizard" was taken off the air in March 1987, and Rappaport was offered no other roles of a similar quality. However talented and well-qualified, dwarf actors like Rappaport generally have to resign themselves to roles as elves and munchkins, or accept costume parts as animals or robots – something Rappaport was apparently reluctant to do. No dwarf has yet been offered the leading part in a mainstream movie.

For his role in "The Wizard," Rappaport found himself being recognized in the street, but was unable to obtain permanent work suitable to his training and talent. Despite his cheeky, cheerful image, he often suffered from depression, and was reportedly having a hard time being such a big star in such a little body (he never grew taller than 3'11). Although he often claimed to have been happy the way he was, and alleged that he'd never had a problem with his short stature, Rappaport confessed to friends that he was deeply depressed at being a dwarf, and at being unable to be taken seriously by the "normal" size starlets he lusted after.

On May 2, 1990, at the age of 39, the pint-sized performer put a gun to his head in Laurel Canyon Park, San

straight to hell

Fernando, and brought his short life to an end. His body is buried in the cemetery at Waltham Abbey, in England.

michael ryan

The tranquil historic market town of Hungerford, Berkshire was an unlikely location for a bloody massacre, but then, the 27-year-old Michael Ryan made an unlikely spree killer. A shy, self-conscious loner who lived at home with his mother and found it difficult to make friends, Ryan's life appeared to revolve around his dog, his car, and his collection of guns. Those who knew him describe a man spoiled by his mother, obsessed by knives and firearms, and living in an elaborately-constructed fantasy world inspired by John Rambo, the character played by Sylvester Stallone in the film *First Blood*.

Although the morning of Wednesday, 19th August 1987 was stiflingly hot, Michael Ryan put on the paramilitary uniform he liked to wear, including combat boots and flak jacket, and armed himself with a selection of weapons from his extensive collection: a Beretta pistol, an M1 carbine and a high-velocity Kalashnikov rifle. He then drove his silver Vauxhall Astra a few miles out of town, into the Savernake Forest in Wiltshire, where the mass bloodshed began.

Ryan's first victim was Susan Godfrey, an attractive, ebullient young mother who was picnicking in the forest with her two small children. Ryan approached Godfrey, separated her from her children, and marched her at gunpoint into the woods, where he fired fifteen high velocity bullets into her back at point-blank range. The children were left unharmed.

After murdering Susan Godfrey, Ryan returned to his car and drove to the Golden Arrow filling station on the A4 at Froxfield, where at 12.40pm he filled up the tank of his car and a five-litre petrol can. Replacing the can in his boot, Ryan lifted out his Kalashnikov AK47 semi-automatic rifle, crouched slightly, raised the butt to his right shoulder, took aim at the cashier – mother-of-three Kakaub Dean – and fired. The shot went wide; Kakaub Dean dropped to the floor and made the first of many panicked calls received that afternoon by the local emergency services. As she was making the call, Ryan entered the service station, walked up to the counter behind which she was hiding and stood over her as she begged for her life. But when he pulled the trigger, nothing happened; the gun was empty. Kakaub Dean had survived.

Next stop for Ryan was 4, South View, his own home, where he shot and killed his devotedly attached mother, then set fire to their house, which burned to a shell. Abandoning his car, Ryan then continued on foot down the suburban street, running and jogging, paramilitary-style, as he gunned down his neighbors at random. On South View, he killed Jack Gibbs, a 66-year-old neighbour, and his invalid wife Myrtle. Then he shot down 70-year-old Roland Mason and his wife Sheila as they come out of the front door of their house at 6, South View. 84-year-old retired shopkeeper Abdur Khan was killed as he was mowing his front lawn.

Ryan then made his way into the center of Hungerford, which was more crowded than usual, since Wednesday was market day, and the weather was fine. Brandishing his weapons, Ryan caused a horrified panic when he rampaged across a busy recreation ground where children were playing on the swings and slides, and people swimming in the outdoor pool. On the other side of the park, he began shooting randomly at the drives of passing cars. George White happened to be driving through the town when he was shot and killed by Ryan. 34-year-old Ian Playle, driving through Hungerford with his wife, Elizabeth, and their two children, was hit by a burst of gunfire and died later in hospital.

Turning into quiet Priory Avenue, Ryan mowed down pedestrian Ken Clements in the street, then murdered 67-year-old Douglas Wainwright at the wheel of his car. Lisa Mildenhall, a 14-year-old schoolgirl playing in her front garden, was hit by four bullets but miraculously survived the ambush. Around the corner in Coldharbor Lane, Francis Butler and Marcus Barnard were not so lucky; the two men both died in a hail of gunfire.

Meanwhile, a flood of phone calls to the emergency services led to the dispatch of two police cars, one of which—driven by P.C. Roger Brereton—was unlucky enough to get in the way of Ryan's AK47, and was hit by twenty-four shots. Before dying, Brereton heroically managed to put in a call asking for serious back-up, which was received by P.C. Jeremy Wood. Wood immediately called for a firearms team, armed response units and a helicopter, set up a series of road blocks, and evacuated picnicking families. But the gunman continued his rampage, turning into Priory Road and killing 22-year-old Sandra Hill in her car.

In just over an hour, Michael Ryan took the lives of sixteen people, and left many others seriously wounded. Shortly before 1.50pm, he entered the John O'Gaunt secondary school, empty for the summer, and the building was quickly surrounded by armed officers. A siege situation rapidly developed, with specialist marksmen and negotiators surrounding the school in an attempt to persuade Ryan to surrender. All telephone lines to Hungerford were shut down, and roads in and out of the town were blocked.

The siege went on for five hours, during which Ryan appeared chillingly lucid, almost reasonable, as he talked to police. His main concern was the fate of his black Labrador; he also wanted to know whether his mother was still alive, or whether his gunfire had killed her on the spot. His intention was clearly to take his own life. "It's funny," he told police at one point. "I've killed all those people, but I haven't got the guts to blow my own brains out."

Nevertheless, at just after 7pm, a muffled shot from inside the building broke the uneasy silence. It was a further three hours before police cautiously entered the school building, with a team of two armed officers covering each other as they dodged from classroom to classroom. Finally, they discovered Michael Ryan, sitting in a corner with a shotgun between his knees, and a bullet in his brain, having finally summoned up the courage to commit the most troublesome of his murders. Ryan's suicide brought an end to a shooting spree that had lasted only a few hours, but claimed the lives of sixteen people, and injured another fourteen.

As Ryan would have been well aware, a shotgun to the head provides the most certain way to die by firearm, with death coming almost instantaneously. In fact, shotgun fire is "overkill," often providing far more power than is necessary to kill a single human being, and usually leaving a terrible mess. After his long hours of hesitation, Ryan clearly chose a method that would virtually guarantee no chance of survival. His funeral took place on 3rd September, 1987, where he was grieved by a total of seven mourners.

adolf hitler

"Twilight of the Gods, come forth from the abyss: night of
nothingness, enshroud the world."
–Richard Wagner, *Götterdämmerung*

"The Führer has it easy. He doesn't have a family to look after.
If the worst comes to the worst in the war, he'll leave us all in
the mess and put a bullet through his head."
–An anonymous German woman in an air-raid shelter in
Schweinfurt, April 1944

Berlin. 30/4/45, 15:30: Two newlyweds celebrate their
honeymoon by taking leave of this world. Gunsmoke and a
strong almond scent fill the suffocating subterranean room where
they died. The fifty-six year old groom slumps on a sofa, a coin-
sized bullet hole seeps blood from his head. A red puddle congeals
on the carpet near his Walther 7.65mm revolver. Beside the pistol
are the bride's shoes, slipped off before curling up to her husband
to bite down on a cyanide capsule.

   The couple are carried up fifty feet of stairs to a
demolished garden. They're dumped in a shallow pit dug in
preparation for hasty obsequies. Petrol is poured on the bodies,
and set alight. Fire consumes the corpses in the makeshift
cremation pyre. The small funeral party raise their arms in salute,
before hurrying back to safety below. A graceless farewell for one
fond of pageantry, but under the circumstances, formalities are
needless.

   Fascination with Hitler's suicide has engendered a cottage

industry rehashing the memories of those peripherally present at the scene. Fear of the potent mythology of these celebrated corpses led the Soviets to destroy the death site, and secretly rebury the corpses, obscuring the facts of the case for over fifty years. Such mystery-mongering inspired legends of Hitler's survival, intermingled with Fourth Reich UFO fantasies. If the JFK hit is modern history's most discussed homicide, the Führer's finale takes pride of place as the suicide of the last century. When Hitler's skull fragments surfaced in a Russian archive, many of the technical enigmas of the case were solved. Rather than offer another forensic postmortem, an autopsy of Hitler's lifelong dance with self-destruction seems more compelling. For suicide looms over Hitler's career like a somber Wagnerian leitmotif foreshadowing the final act.

As a dreamy adolescent in provincial Austria, he threatened to drown himself when a local beauty named Stefanie ignored his admiration from afar. This intertwining of suicide with romance cast a morbid pall over many of Hitler's later liaisons. During World War I, Hitler's comrades wondered if the moody loner's bravery in combat was his way of daring death.

The fledgling Führer threatened suicide again during the November 8 November 1923 Putsch. The obscure agitator seized his audience's attention at a beerhall nationalist meeting by firing his revolver at the ceiling, then pointing his pistol to his forehead, shouting,"If I am not victorious by tomorrow afternoon, I'm a dead man!" Ordering a march for the next morning, he declared,"If it all comes off, all's well, if not, we'll hang ourselves." The demonstration was disrupted by police fire, but Hitler escaped to supporter Ernst Hanfstaengl's home. When police surrounded the house, he again swore to shoot himself before he could be taken prisoner. Frau Hanfstaengl wrested the gun away from him, tossing it into a flour barrel.

In 1931, the love of Hitler's life, his young niece, Geli Raubal, died in his Munich flat – officially a suicide. Rumors circulated that Hitler himself shot Geli during a lover's spat, or that he'd ordered her execution. Hitler fell into a major depression after Geli's death, requiring his associates to keep suicide watch over him. Hitler returned ferociously to the political fray, but periods of gloom plagued him ever after. A hypochondriac Hitler fretted that little time was left to complete his mission. In 1932, confronted with a leadership battle with left-wing Nazi Gregor Strasser, Hitler told Goebbels: "If the Party collapses, I'll put an end to it in five minutes with my pistol." Hitler so repeatedly invoked the scenario that he ultimately enacted – a self-inflicted shot to the head – that his fate seems almost inevitable.

Other women Hitler was linked with fell prey to his suicidal aura. Actress Renate Müller died after jumping from a sanitarium window. British fascist Unity Mitford sustained brain damage after shooting herself in 1939. Lovelorn Eva Braun attempted two trial runs before she succeeded in 1945.

After attaining power, Der Führer prophesied that he wouldn't attain "the ripe old age of the ordinary citizen." His gambler's life, hurtling from crisis to crisis, was guided by the motto *Weltmacht oder Niedergang!* – world conquest or downfall. A thousand year victory or total failure – Hitler's Manichean *Weltanschauung* brooked no half measures. The obstinacy inspiring Germans to take faith in his iron will was also a personal handicap, plunging him into desperation when thwarted. Joachim Fest described "Hitler's sensitive nervous system", a "strange alternation of moods, first apathy, then violent despair".

The feverish pace of his reconstruction and rearmament program, and the breathless tempo at which he waged war was a race against his own mortality. In 1939, death-haunted Hitler proclaimed, "We may be destroyed, but if we are, we shall drag a world with us – a world in flames."

Hitler's private conversation during the war reveals that he imagined a heroic afterlife :"I shall feel I am in my proper place if after my death I find myself, together with others like me, on some sort of Olympus. I shall be in the company of the most enlightened spirits of all time." He speculated that ,"The elements of which our body is made belong to the cycle of nature; and as for our soul, it's possible that it might return to limbo, until it gets an opportunity to reincarnate itself." During one of the all-night soliloquies insomniac Hitler expected his intimates to endure, he ruminated: "I advise the desperate man to have patience for one year unless the desire to commit suicide is due to a lover's quarrel."

When Stalingrad commander von Paulus failed to shoot himself after defeat, Hitler scorned his cowardice: "What does 'life' mean? Life is the nation; the individual must die. What remains alive beyond the individual is the nation." He wondered, "How can anyone be afraid of that second in which he can free himself from misery?... It is only a fraction of a second, and then you are freed from all of that, and you have quiet and eternal peace."

After 1943, Hitler retreated into solipsistic reclusion, seen only by his staff in headquarters far from the bombing devastating Germany. When traveling by day, Hitler closed the blackout curtains in his armored train – he preferred not to see the shattered cities. Hitler fantasized that secret weapons could turn the tide, or that his foes would betray each other.

By the time of his return to Berlin, in January, 1945, the battle for the shrinking Reich was all but lost. Built to serve as the enduring centerpiece of his millennial empire, his Chancellery's classical grandeur was a bombed-out facade. The exhausted fifty-five year old shuffled down the staircase into a labyrinthine bunker deep beneath the ruins. He never saw another sunrise or sunset.

Hitler would barely have been recognized as the charismatic visionary once hailed by millions. The Greeks, who he admired as the pinnacle of Aryan civilization, would have said that here was a man whose *daimon* had departed. The famous forelock of brown hair and mustache were gray, the steely blue eyes now glazed, staring dolefully into space. His face was puffy, tinged yellow-gray. The voice that galvanized a nation was now a weary monotone.

His posture sagged, bowed forward in an old man's stoop. Since the failed 1944 assassination attempt, his left arm and leg trembled violently. Peter Hartmann, Hitler's bodyguard, remembered that on his Führer's macabre final birthday, "He seemed closer to seventy-six than fifty-six. He looked what I would call physically senile". In the last days, saliva drooled from his lips, food soiling his uniform.

The cramped existence Hitler led in the Bunker, scuttling under low ceilings and through narrow passageways like a passenger on a sinking submarine, was the lowest point he'd ever reached. The Wolf's final lair was a stale-aired crypt of drab unplastered walls, moist and clammy to the touch. A stifling odor of latrines and anxiety prevailed. Dust clouds fell from the walls as artillery pummeled the skeletal city overhead.

If he could not survive the war, Hitler was determined that Germany itself should not survive. On 19 March, he issued his "Nero" order, commanding Armaments Minister Speer to destroy "all military, transportation, communications, industrial and supply facilities, as well as all resources within the Reich." Speer described this as an "application of the scorched earth principle in its most sweeping form... how was it possible, I thought, that one man wanted to transform this land into a desert?" Speer sabotaged the order.

Propaganda Minister Goebbels sought to bolster Hitler's morale with comparisons to Frederick the Great's victory when faced with seeming defeat. Roosevelt's death on April 13, 1945 was viewed in the Bunker as a miracle. The celebration was short-lived; the enemy wasn't slowed for a second. On April 15, Eva Braun arrived unbidden, pledging to stand by her man.

Straight to hell

On 20 April, his birthday, Hitler glimpsed the world above for the last time. A few pitiful teenage soldiers gathered to greet the Leader, who mumbled hollow words of encouragement. He could no longer instill the confidence he once conjured in fanatic crowds. He descended again, ordering his generals to deploy non-existent phantom armies.

On April 22, a last-ditch counter-attack failed. Hitler threw the pencils he used to mark maps in the air, ranting against *Luftwaffe* incompetence and *Wehrmacht* treachery. Hitler shouted, "That's the end! Under such circumstances I cannot direct anything anymore! The war is lost! But you are mistaken, gentlemen, if you think that I will leave Berlin! I'd rather put a bullet though my head!"

Bolsheviks and Jews would "not parade his corpse as a trophy", he fumed. Then Hitler became calmer than he'd been in years. His decision to die nullified the agitation of the last year's downward spiral. His loyal staff volunteered to stay on until the end, although Hitler encouraged them to abandon the Bunker. Shortly thereafter, Hitler learned that Göring and Himmler had betrayed him, seeking surrender terms, each hoping to fill the sudden vacuum of power by succeeding him as Führer. Hitler stripped them of their offices, a hollow gesture under the circumstances.

As the Soviets pushed closer, Hitler considered leading the last stand in the streets with a rifle, but the risk of capture was too great. Goebbels, his wife, and their six young children moved in to die with the Leader. Now all talk centered on efficient suicide techniques. Cyanide was tested on the Führer's beloved German Shepherd and her puppies; their killing presaged the poisoning of the Goebbels six children shortly after Hitler's death.

On April 29, after midnight, Hitler married Eva, acknowledging for posterity the woman who'd served as his secret mistress since 1932. Fittingly, this civil ceremony *Liebestod* was officiated by a city administrator named Wagner.

During a bleak reception, Hitler recalled the Goebbels' wedding years earlier: "What a contrast! For me, marriage and death are to be more closely linked in time." After the joyless celebration, he dictated his Last Will and Testament: "I will not fall into the hands of an enemy who requires a new spectacle, exhibited by the Jews, to divert his whipped-up masses. I have therefore decided to remain in Berlin, and there to choose death voluntarily at the moment when I believe that the residency of the Führer and Chancellor can no longer be held... My wife and I choose to die in order to escape the shame of overthrow or capitulation. It is our wish for our bodies to be cremated immediately on the place where I have performed the greater part of my daily work during twelve years of service to my people."

After one hour's sleep, Hitler awakened, appointing Admiral Dönitz as Führer. Goebbels was awarded with the title of Reichs Chancellor, an empty glory considering that the Reich now consisted of a few blocks surrounding the Bunker. Eva made her way up to the garden where she would soon be cremated for one last look at the sun.

News of the execution of Mussolini and his mistress by Communists strengthened Hitler's resolve to act quickly. After handing out cyanide to the staff, the Hitlers shook hands silently with the faithful, withdrawing into their quarters.

Soviet artillery pounded directly above. A loud gunshot resounded in the Bunker. Young Hellmut Goebbels looked up from playing with his siblings – "Sounds like a direct hit!"

Post-war propaganda paints Hitler's suicide as a coward's act. It's better understood as a final control over a fate that no longer obeyed his internal vision. The Christian edict against suicide seeks to prevent man from destroying God's creation. Through willed self-destruction, the lapsed Catholic Hitler sought to affirm his role as martyred messiah of the German world-soul. The indignities of trial and execution as a war criminal would have robbed him of the authorship of his carefully stage-managed myth. Hitler engineered his suicide as a melodramatic Golgotha, the self-sacrifice in flames of St. Adolf. If he is largely remembered as an evil avatar whose utopia – like all utopias – was never realized, who can deny that he succeeded in at least one of his stated aims:

"I know how to keep my hold on people after I have passed on – my life shall not end in the mere form of death. It will, on the contrary, begin then."

guy debord

In his rural retreat at Champot in the Haute Loire départment of France, on the 30th of November, 1994, Guy Debord shot himself in the heart. That, at least, represents the version of events hoisted up by the fleet of obituaries launched in the turbulent wake of his demise. I want to take another tack and locate the deed which resulted in Debord's death at a distance of some forty two years and four hundred kilometres from its official time and place.

No picture of the life of Guy Debord could ever offer more than a blurred snapshot of its itinerant intensities. Despite episodes of ostensible inertia, his was a life distinguished by movement. Movement between artistic, political and social milieus: involvement in the Lettriste group's post-Surrealist provocations in the boulevards and the bookshops of the 1950s; inauguration and subsequent domination of the Situationist International, the faction charged with a catalytic role in the uprisings of Paris '68; participation in Europe's dissident underground in the 70's and 80's, a role which attracted spurious rumours of CIA recruitment, Moscow gold, associations with terrorist cells, even implication in the murder of his publisher, Gérard Lebovici; and, in the 1990s, gradual elevation through elite acclaim, neither sought nor particularly welcomed, to a reputation as a supreme literary stylist. Movement, too, around private relationships that seemed either to flare into fire and then fall into ashes or to smoulder with inextinguishable love or implacable hatred. Movement, finally, as a fundamental theme across his creative endeavours: acerbic essayist, editor of an influential journal, eccentric autobiographer, film-maker whose forty years of works constitute a compelling and corrosive anti-cinema, translator, co-inventor of The Game of War – a military strategy simulation which he feared "may be the only one of my works that anyone will dare acknowledge as having some value" – and author of one of the enduring oppositional texts of the twentieth century, The Society of the Spectacle.

Given the errant movement of his personal life, Guy Debord's theoretical perspective was, by contrast, relatively static. Debord arrived very early on at a sophisticated diagnosis of the malady of the modern world that, subject to subtle refinement, persisted until his end. At the risk of crude caricature, his position can be condensed into a critique of the contemporary world – its alleged diversity of buildings, commodities, media and 'ideologies' – as the material manifestation of one single programme, that of the destruction of the lived life. The name that Debord attaches to this world, one that has stuck, is that of the spectacle. "The spectacle in its generality is a concrete inversion of life, and, as such, the autonomous movement of non-life" . The spectacle is the "absolute denial of life, in the shape of a fallacious paradise, [that is] no longer projected onto the heavens, but finds its place instead within the material life itself". In place of genuine life – 'la vie vite' of the Situationist graffiti on the walls of Paris – the spectacle promotes instead a somnambulant non-life that is as economically productive as it is normatively conformist. "The spectacle is the bad dream of modern society in chains, expressing nothing more than its wish for sleep. The spectacle is the guardian of that sleep".

If the spectacle is that which is resolutely opposed to life then perhaps there is something contradictory or even something complicit in Guy Debord volunteering to take his own? This potential problem is rendered yet more acute to the extent that Debord determined to erase any gap between his theoretical avowals and his everyday practices. "Chateaubriand pointed out

– and rather precisely, all told: 'Of the modern French authors of my time, I am the only one whose life is true to his works'. In any case, I have certainly lived as I have said one should, and this was perhaps even more unusual among the people of my time". Again, "[i]f certain people have so much enjoyed my style, it is because of the examples of my life". Answers need to be sought not in Champot in 1994 but at another geographical and historical juncture – in Paris, in 1952.

Returning to 1952 might seem like a bizarre tactic, yet buried in Debord's texts are invitations to follow precisely this lead. Instead of tracing his notoriety to the events of '68 or anything that followed, he suggests that "I think rather that it is what I did in 1952 that has been disliked for so long". 1952 marked the point at which Guy Debord broke definitively from his familial background, allowed any opportunities to pursue formal education to slip away, and immersed himself instead in a certain Paris. This was not the somewhat earnest atmosphere which Sartre, De Beauvoir and their acolytes installed in the *Les Deux Magots* café but a ruder culture that drifted between the drinking dens of Chez Moineau, Le Mabillon, L'Old Navy, La Pergola and Le Tonneau D'Or. It was in this superficially unpromising environment that Debord set out to find "the 'North-West Passage' of the geography of real life", a way beyond the constraints of what was to be called the spectacle.

Ultimately, the most evocative portrait of this expedition derives not from Debord's own pen or indeed that of his Situationist fellow travellers but from a Dutch photographer, Ed Van Der Elsken. Van Der Elsken was drawn into the same magnetic territory and published two documentary projects on the area, *Paris! 1950 – 1954* and *Love on the Left Bank*. The latter book weaves images into the fabric of a semi-fictional narrative, where names are changed and incidents embellished but where the rich flavours of the time and place are nevertheless presented in pungent detail. "I stayed in the quartier. I learned that Ann's friends lived by their wits. Mostly they begged. They stole a little, they got themselves kept by another boy or girl, they dealt in hashish. Or they worked in Les Halles for a night, carrying baskets and cases. For the rest they were underfed. So they made ends meet. Dinner was a piece of bread eaten on the street. At night you could swipe milk bottles left on the pavement outside dairies. For thirty francs you could get chips at the Place De L'Odéon. When the going was good you might blow a hundred francs on a meat-ball or spaghetti Levantin ...You could sleep in cafés, on a bench in the Luxembourg, or in parked cars in the Place Saint Sulpice. During the day you could sleep in the cinema or the métro. When you had a new girlfriend you stood yourself to a room in a hotel".

Missing from this particular recipe, however, is one of its most important ingredients, that of alcohol. Elsewhere in his two works, Van Der Elsken proves himself a worthy witness to this dimension, portraying rooms fogged with tobacco fumes, where glasses and bottles reign in varying states of emptiness and the cafés' patrons reel in varying states of inebriation, their eyes sparkling during the initial euphoria, dulling as the consumption increases and finally closing as limits are exceeded. "The owner of one of the bistros said, 'These boys are not so bad'. And she cleaned up their vomit".

It seems that Debord's North-West Passage was hidden somewhere within this zone of intoxication that opened up in Paris in 1952. Although Debord ruefully conceded that "Never again will we drink so young', the uniqueness of the adventure bequeathed to its participants a strange inheritance, a compulsion to "discover how to live the days that came after in a manner worthy of such a fine beginning. You want to prolong that first experience of illegality for ever".

Moralists amongst us may baulk at assigning a pivotal role to drink and drunkenness but Guy Debord displayed little coyness in this regard. "I also like good wine and, at least in this area, I have generally kept myself within the bounds of excess". At times, a note of stubborn pride enters his confessions. "Among the small number of things that I have liked and know how to do well, what I have assuredly known how to do best is drink. Even though I have read a lot, I have drunk even more. I have written much less than most people who write; but I have drunk much more than most people who drink".

Understanding Debord's dedication to drink perhaps involves establishing parallels with other writers' engagements with substances that supposedly offer access to other realms: Alfred Jarry's ether, De Quincey, Coleridge and Cocteau's opium, Castenada's peyote, Huxley's mescaline, Gregory Bateson and Timothy Leary's LSD, Kerouac's benzedrine, Benjamin and Baudelaire's hashish. Yet drink lacks the exotic charm of these other stimulants and Debord's commitment to it had nothing of the 'tourist' approach that afforded a cheap holiday in other people's misery from which to return, suitably altered, to a creative sobriety.

Swallowing the next shot was not, however, an end in itself for Debord. Booze did represent a vehicle which could, with care, transport its user to other destinations. For one thing, its consumption functioned as a measure of the passing days and decades. "The sensation of time slipping by has always been a keen one for me, and I have been attracted by it as others are attracted by the void, or by water". For another, it acted as an excellent accomplice in the avoidance of the productive existence. "A doctor of nothing, I have firmly kept myself apart from all semblance of participation in the circles that then passed for intellectual or artistic. I admit that my merit in this respect was well tempered by my great laziness, as well as by my very meagre capacities for confronting the work of such careers". Consequently, alcohol was enlisted, from 1952 onwards, as a strategic aide-de-camp in Debord's war on the spectacle's non-life.

Nonetheless, drink operated as a double agent. Its effects

may well have assisted Debord's aristocratic refusal yet they simultaneously eroded his own biological integrity. Debord's final, magnificent, film was a collaboration with the journalist Brigitte Cornand commissioned by Canal Plus and entitled *Guy Debord: Son Art Et Son Temps*. Broadcast on television on 9 Jan, 1995, just over a month after his death, an on-screen text referring to Debord, "Illness called alcoholic polyneuritis; first signs appeared in autumn 1990. At first almost imperceptible, but progressive. Became truly distressing in late November 1994. With all incurable diseases, there is much to be gained by neither seeking nor accepting medical care. This is the opposite of an illness that you contract through an unfortunate lack of prudence. On the contrary, contracting it requires determination over a whole lifetime".

Obviously, the proximity of extreme alcohol use and fatality was not something that had only occurred to Debord at the end. Indeed, the correlation had been addressed during the first, fateful attempt on the North-West Passage in 1952. "Not far from Chez Moineau, there was a famous government information poster which warned that 'L'alcool tue lentement' (Alcohol kills slowly). The poster had not been up for twenty-four hours when, on Debord's instructions, a raiding party from Chez Moineau had scrawled over it: 'On s'en fout. On a le temps'. ('We don't give a fuck. We've got the time').

Considering his consciousness of the connection between drink and death, is it stretching things too far to suggest that Debord's suicide occurred not with the instaneity of a pistol shot in 1994 but with the prolonged unfolding of a way of life which was begun in Paris, 1952 and whose ultimate conclusion was perhaps no less certain? Irrespective of whether this argument is sustainable, what is clear is that, for Debord, suicide is by no means a capitulation to the spectacle. Far from it, the society of the spectacle works hard to banish any active contemplation of death. "Immobilised at the distorted centre of the movement of its world, the consciousness of the spectator can have no sense of an individual life moving towards self-realisation, or toward death. Someone who has given up the idea of living life will surely never be able to embrace death" .

Thus, just as non-life is not necessarily synonymous with death, then, for Debord, suicide may itself be strangely allied to life. If the "social absence of death is at one with the social absence of life", then valorising death might correspondingly bestow value to the authentic, active life which the spectacle seeks everywhere and in every way to cheapen. That this position appears paradoxical would by no means unsettle Debord. Indeed, Debord's early fascination with suicide led him to script the following statement in his first film, aired in auspicious year of 1952, "My little sister, look at the state we're in ... The Isère and misery go on. We are powerless. The perfection of suicide is in ambiguity". After all, as he and Alice Becker Ho established in their board game, "The Game of War, like war itself and all forms of thought or strategic action, tends to impose at each instant, considerations of contradictory necessities. Each side, to the extent that it knew how to keep its freedom of manoeuvre, finds itself constrained to choose between operations in which it lacks sufficient means in space and time".

End games are frequently the most fraught stages of any military campaign. The classical philosophers of conflict – Clausewitz, Machiavelli, Sun Tzu – who Debord drew upon in his life are strangely quiet when it comes to bringing hostilities to a close and fall completely silent when it comes to addressing defeat itself. Perhaps, however, to speak of defeat in relation to Debord's demise is to misunderstand the rules of engagement for his protracted assault on the spectacle's non-life. I don't think that Debord avoided defeat by seeking infamy beyond the grave as his biographer Len Bracken claims, "[o]nly his suicide, his final creative act of destruction, seemed designed to stun the mass of spectators into recognising his worth". Debord was just as contemptuous of those who could be identified as spectators – why sacrifice his life to the undead? – as he was disdainful of any public recognition of his worth – why seek meagre crumbs of posthumous attention from a world which has "never hidden its intense revulsion when speaking about me, as well as anything that resembles me"? Indeed, as Debord's lover and collaborator, Alice Becker Ho argued, "Guy did not have to die, it was a clear choice he made. He refused to be defeated by illness, or the world which was making him a famous man of letters. He wished simply not to be present when that happened". It may well be the case that Guy Debord would never have had to make his fatal choice had he not first embarked upon the voyage of intoxication in Paris, in 1952. However, had he not gone in search of the North-West Passage with such ardour, he might never have found intimations of life beyond the reaches of the spectacle; he and his comrades might never have discovered an uncertain victory in the ambiguity of suicide where others, less adventurous perhaps, would only experience defeat. "Many have dreamed up republics and principalities which have never in truth been known to exist; the gulf between how one should live and how one does live is so wide that a man who neglects what is actually done for what should be done learns the way to self-destruction rather than self-preservation".

harry crosby

"I want a long straight road into the Sun and a car with the cut out wide open speeding a mile a minute into the Sun with a princess by my side"
–Harry Crosby

"I want to make a poem of my life" –Yukio Mishima

Harry Crosby's life burned with an incandescent white-heat, and his suicide was an affirmation of his quasi-Nietzschean mystical beliefs. In Crosby the destructive spirit was not an annihilator but, through a uniquely dialectical perversion, a liberator. A death well chosen was, for Crosby, not a negative gesture, but rather a resounding affirmation, a "yes" carried into the abyss. For Crosby, death was the final and greatest of many adventures.

Born into a conservative Boston family on June 4th, 1898, it was expected that Harry Crosby would work in banking, marry correctly, sire an appropriate heir, and retire to a suitable New England – or at least East Coast – town. When the teenage Crosby volunteered for service in the blood and shit soaked, cadaver strewn trenches of Northern Europe during the First World War, he was still primarily doing what was expected. The experience as an ambulance driver would be character building in the eyes of his family.

In the churned rotting mud of the Second Battle of Verdum, Crosby had the task of hauling the wretched casualties, and often corpses, from the frontline to the American Field Army section. On some days Crosby would drag more than two-hundred-and-fifty blasted, shot, stabbed, and destroyed bodies to the field hospitals. This was a truly charnel landscape, more grotesque than those realized in previous conflicts, as men on horseback would battle heavy artillery, where bayonets and hand to hand combat would be used alongside tanks, in these battlefields the atavism of previous conflicts met the mechanized terror of modern warfare. The world was turned upside down, and nothing was left unscathed.

On November 22nd, 1917, Crosby was driving an ambulance, loaded with brutally wounded soldiers, when a shell exploded only feet away. By some insane miracle Crosby escaped all injury, but his ambulance and its grisly flesh cargo were annihilated. Death's steed had ridden past Crosby.

Harry Crosby should have died.

In surviving the slaughter he became obsessed with his own death. It is unsurprising that he would come to know this date as his death-day and would mark it annually in his diaries and with rituals of his own design.

Following his military service – during which Crosby also carried the wounded at the Battle of Orme for which he was awarded the Croix de Guerre – he returned to Boston, and Harvard. He was expected to settle down, but his experiences of conflict, and growing passion for literature, meant the young man had other plans.

On July 4th, 1920, Crosby met the woman who would become his soul-mate and the major inspiration for the rest of his life: Polly Peabody. Seven years his senior, Polly was married to Richard Roger Peabody and was the mother of two children. The marriage was unsatisfactory, however, and the young Crosby began a campaign for Polly's heart, declaring his love for her only hours after their first meeting. In a grim warning of what was to come Harry threatened suicide if the relationship was not formalized – as he wrote "I'll... kill you and then myself so that we can go right to Heaven together". Polly was Harry's "religion" and he declared that "whenever you want we shall die together".

The Crosby / Peabody relationship was scandalous, but Polly began divorce proceedings, and the couple were married eight months after her divorce. The two lovers – stifled by the conservatism of their Boston families – moved to Paris during their courtship. In Paris the couple lived exceptionally well, surviving on their familial incomes and the benefits of the exchange rate.

In France the couple were able to pursue their passions fully; literature, poetry, and decadence. Harry began to wear a black flower in his lapel, effecting the appearance of a noir-dandy, a black mirror to the classic / clichéd image of the 'colourful character'. In Paris, Harry was also able to fully consolidate his own cosmology based on sun worship. Such was his religious conviction in the power of the Sun, Crosby had the image of the black-sun tattooed onto his back, and a cross and a pagan sun sign tattooed onto the soles of his feet; here was a man possessed by his own unique synchretic religion. Crosby's beliefs emerged from a combination of sources; they acknowledged the influence of the magical interpretations of the Sun that emerged from Ancient cultures and indigenous peoples, but combined these interpretations with a loosely Nietzschean understanding of the universe as will and as affirmation. The Sun represents dynamic, vital existence, the essence of life, energy, as well as the solar eruption of limitless energy and primordial expenditure. When Harry read Nietzsche's *Thus Spake Zarathustra* he was particularly inspired by the command that one must "die at the right time", and the Crosbys set a date for their joint suicide: Halloween, 1942 – although whether this was a realistic proposal, or merely a lover's discourse remains open to interpretation.

The Crosbys' passion for literature informed their days, both wrote poetry and kept journals. Harry in particular produced numerous volumes of poetry. In 1924, while preparing a book of her poetry entitled *Crosses Of Gold* for publication Polly

straight to hell

was debating the use of a penname, and after much debate, Harry suggested she become 'Caresse Crosby'. It was the name by which he would know her for the rest of his life.

In 1927 their passion for literature drove Harry and Caresse to found their own publishing company, and the couple established Black Sun Press – the title of the company representing their fascination with the Sun and Harry's mystical beliefs. The company would publish works not just by Caresse and Harry but also key literary figures such as James Joyce, D.H. Lawrence, Hart Crane, Ezra Pound, and Kay Boyle, amongst others. Each edition would be designed by the Crosbys and represented their belief in the importance of their literary and publishing project. Thus literature too retained a mystical importance to Harry.

In 1928 Harry Crosby inherited a massive library of an estimated eight-thousand books, from Walter Berry. These books included an illuminated Koran, a Gutenberg Bible, first editions by Baudelaire and Voltaire, and The Book of the Dead. Yet, even as he inherited this epic library, Crosby began to understand that books weighed him down, thus he spent days disposing of his inheritance; leaving invaluable ancient editions hidden amongst the clutter of second hand books stalls and book shops, and handing first editions to people on the street. Crosby was circulating literature, but he was also paring down his library, with the idea that, having handed everything unnecessary away he would be left with the most important books. The gesture was one of logocentric mayhem.

Harry Crosby's other interest was decadence. He embraced the ritual of opium smoking, absinth drinking, and hashish consumption. Harry enjoyed gambling, and the couple owned a racehorse. He took numerous lovers - seducing them with a passion similar to that with which he won Polly Peabody's heart, but he always returned to his true love: Caresse. The love burning brighter and with an intensity more ferocious than before. Harry's lovers / sexual conquests were often other decadents from a similar social circle, although he did indulge in one documented homosexual affair with an Arab boy known as Bakhara. With the flourish of the true literary libertine he also fell in love with a woman known as the Grey Princess; named Jacqueline she was the perfect woman, except she did not exist, representing merely an unattainable desire to Harry, she was nothing other than a liminal hymn.

Harry was also influenced by modern art and modern technologies, and he began to take photographs, producing pictures that were abstracted forms taken from the engines of racing cars and planes. Already a keen driver, flight increasingly obsessed Crosby, and he began to take flying lessons. Flight enabled travel, but more importantly for Harry it enabled one to get closer to the heavens, closer to God, and – like Icarus – closer to the Sun.

By the end of the twenties Harry's life was a furious combination of ritualized worship, flying lessons, publishing, writing, and decadent excesses. In 1928, in an attempt to create a space in which to calm down, away from the excesses of Paris, Harry and Caresse rented a Mill House in the French countryside, but this too became a zone of excess, with banquets and parties occurring frequently and guests including not just writers and poets but also artists and celebrities – both Salvador Dali and Douglas Fairbanks were guests at the country retreat.

Then, in July 1928, Harry met Josephine Noyes Rotch. As usual Harry seduced Josephine with familiar declarations of undying love and passion, but this time his purpose was grimly serious. Rotch married Albert Bigelow in 1929, but despite her marriage she maintained a relationship with the tattooed poet.

It was in New York that the final suicidal affirmation occurred. Harry had a clandestine meeting with Josephine in the studio of Stanley Mortimer. Here he asserted his faith in the universe.

straight to hell

Harry and Josephine were found in a slumbered embrace, both had single bullet holes in their foreheads, in his hand Harry still held the gun that killed them. It is believed that Harry shot Josephine, then lay next to her cadaver for two hours – presumably contemplating the magnitude of this poetic gesture and supreme philosophical affirmation – before turning the gun on himself. It was December 10th, 1929.

Two days later Crosby's corpse was cremated. It is uncertain what happened to the ashes, which were taken by Caresse, although it is known that Harry once declared he would like them to be scattered from a plane flying over New York City.

In the final analysis Crosby's suicide must be viewed as an act of affirmation, of will, and as an attempt to control and master his own destiny, his own death.

Bibliography:

Chris Mikul, *Bizarrism: Strange Lives, Cults, Celebrated Lunacy*, Stockport: Critical Vision, 1999.

Geoffrey Wolff, *Black Sun: The Brief Transit and Violent Eclipse Of Harry Crosby*, New York: Random House, 1976.

Internet:

http://www.english.uiuc.edu/maps/poets/a_f/crosby/crosby.htm

john mccollum

In October 1984, confused nineteen-year-old heavy metal fan John Daniel McCollum committed suicide by blasting himself in the head with a shotgun after allegedly listening to various songs by Ozzy Osbourne, most notably "Suicide Solution". His body was still wearing stereo headphones when it was discovered. "Suicide Solution" includes the lyrics "Evil thoughts and evil doings / Cold, alone, you hang in ruins / Thought that you'd escape the reaper / You can't escape the Master Keeper / ... Suicide is the only way out." The coroner's report read "decedent committed suicide by shooting self in head with .22-caliber pistol while listening to devil music."

Although his son was known to have a history of psychiatric difficulties and drug problems, McCollum's father sued Osbourne and his record company, stipulating that Osbourne's music was a proximate cause of his son's suicide, and arguing that Osbourne and his distributors were guilty of negligence, product liability, and intentional misconduct. The case, McCollum vs. CBS, Inc., became an important legal precedent in the U.S. in its confirmation that musical lyrics cannot be construed to contain "requisite call to action" sufficient to strip them of First Amendment protection.

McCollum's prosecution team hired The Institute for Bio-Acoustics Research, Inc. (IBAR) to evaluate "Suicide Solution." Not surprisingly, IBAR found subliminal lyrics that weren't included in the lyric sheet. According to IBAR, the subliminal lyrics are sung at one and a half times the normal rate of speech, and cannot be grasped by the first-time listener.

However, they claim that the subliminal lyrics "are audible enough that their meaning and true intent becomes clear after being listened to over and over again." IBAR claimed that the "subliminal" lyrics in "Suicide Solution" apparently include "Why try, why try? Get the Gun and try it! Shoot... shoot...shoot... do it... do it" followed by the requisite "hideous laughter."

IBAR's analysis of "Suicide Solution" also found the presence of so-called "hemisync tones," which apparently result from "a patented process that uses sound waves to influence an individual's mental state. The tones have been found to increase the rate at which the human brain assimilates and processes information." IBAR alleged that these hemisync tones made nineteen-year-old John McCollum more vulnerable to Ozzy's "suggestive lyrics." According to McCollum's father, "they know what they are putting out … there are people who are out there trying to make money, and they have no hesitation to sell your kids down the drain … you see a perfectly normal kid who doesn't show any signs of depression at all … Then, six hours later, he's dead. Nobody can explain it. The only thing we know is that he was listening to this music." The McCollums' attorney claims he received "at least 20 phone calls from parents indicating that their kids committed suicide...not just listening to rock music, but specifically to Ozzy Osbourne."

"Hemisync tones" seem to be the sonic equivalent of the much-ballyhooed superstition of "subliminal flashes" in film. This myth about the evil power of the media is often perpetuated by the leaders of the Christian right. Billy Graham, for example, claims that "evil" exists within the celluloid print of the movie The Exorcist. The great proponent of "subliminal images" is Wilson Bryan Key, whose book Subliminal Seduction explains how we are constantly surrounded by such messages, including the word "sex" written over and over again on the surface of Ritz Crackers.

Christian groups hostile to rock music often like to point out that the now-infamous California mass murderer Richard Ramirez, the "Night Stalker," was reportedly led into his obsession with the occult and ritual murder through the music of groups like AC/DC. A school friend alleged that their song "Night Prowler" seemed particularly to effect Ramirez. On the record cover of AC/DC's *Highway To Hell*, the album that includes the song "Night Prowler," the singer of the song wears a pentagram round his neck. The most common of satanic symbols, it became Ramirez's calling card, appearing on the walls of his victims' homes, and sometimes on the bodies of victims themselves.

McCollum's case was soundly defeated; the court decided that, like fictional prose and poetry, rock music lyrics are not meant to be taken literally or taken at face value, arguing that although Osbourne's songs may have painted life as a grim reality with suicide being one alternative to the pain of suffering of reality, the music did not in any way specifically intend to encourage listeners to kill themselves. The defense pointed out that were it actually possible to conceal subliminal commands in rock lyrics, it would make far more sense for such commands to induce listeners to buy more of the group's records than to kill themselves.

The case is constantly used as a legal precedent to dismiss similar cases that are regularly brought against the media by shocked and baffled parents, unable to believe that their child might actually have been a rational agent in their suicide. In December 1985, for example, bereaved parents brought action against Judas Priest, claiming the group's lyrics were responsible for a double suicide.

According to the plaintiffs, after listening to the Judas Priest song "Beyond The Realms Of Death," 18-year-olds Raymond Belknap and James Vance went to a nearby church playground, where Belknap put a sawed-off shotgun to his head, pulled the trigger and literally blew his head off. As Belknap lay

Straight to hell

dead on the pavement, Vance took his turn. He said "there was just tons of blood. It was like the gun had grease on it. There was so much blood I could barely handle it, and I reloaded it and then, you know, it was my turn, and I readied myself. I was thinking about all that there was to live for, so much of your life is right before your eyes, and it was like I didn't have any control … my body was compelled to do it and I went ahead and shot."

Vance survived the gunshot wound, but slipped into a coma in November 1988 and died a few days later. The lawsuit argued that "the suggestive lyrics combined with the continuous beat and rhythmic non-changing intonation of the music combined to induce, encourage, aid, abet and mesmerize the plaintiff into believing the answer to life was death." The case was overturned.

A similar case in 1990, Watters vs. TSR, Inc., rejected liability on the part of the manufacturers of *Dungeons And Dragons*, a game alleged to have caused the plaintiff's son to commit suicide. The court decided that holding media companies responsible for the suicide "stretches the concept of forseeability beyond all reason", adding that the plaintiffs were improperly trying to treat "intangible thoughts, ideas and messages contained within the products" as if they were products themselves.

Troubled teenagers will always commit suicide, and baffled parents will always try to impute responsibility to causes beyond the immediate circumstances of their children's daily lives. Scapegoats generally include those demons of youth culture – sex, drugs and rock'n'roll. Perhaps the most archetypal case is that of Diane Linkletter, whose father blamed his daughter's suicide solely on the insidious influence of LSD, even though Diane had repeatedly made clear that her depression had legitimate roots in genuine difficulties, not least of which was her relationship with her father. When faced with the trauma of a teenage suicide, parents are liable to go to extreme lengths to avoid facing the fact that their child may have had legitimate

46

reasons to prefer death to life, and those reasons may well include their feelings about their parents.

Ozzy Osbourne has explained how the song "Suicide Solution," far from being an incitement to suicide, was actually written to mourn the suicide of a close friend. Ironically, thanks to the popular reality show "The Osbournes," currently a cult hit on MTV, Osbourne has been revealed as not the bat-biting, Satan-worshipping Prince of Darkness his reputation might have led us to suspect, but as a teetotal, vegetarian family man devoted to his teenage children and pushed around by his bossy wife.

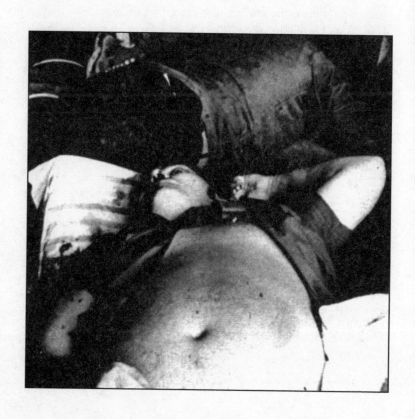

jim jones

In the winter of 1978, Sunday newspapers around the world were ruffled by the news of the mass suicide of 993 people at an American religious commune set in the heart of the jungle in Guyana, South America.

The People's Temple – a Christian religious sect from the United States – were led by the enigmatic Reverend Jim Jones, who had moved his congregation to Guyana from San Francisco a year earlier to escape investigations into his ministry by numerous journalists and politicians. Jones, who had earlier enjoyed the support of Vice President Walter Mondale and First Lady Carolyn Carter for his work with ethnic minorities, the unemployed and animals, had become convinced that Godless America had decided to discredit him because of his socialist beliefs. He'd also become sure that the U.S.A was destined for nuclear war, and convinced his followers that the greenery of South America was the ideal Garden of Eden in which to re-start the world.

It all started to go wrong when John and Grace Stone left the Temple, and entered into a custody battle with Jones over their five-year-old son, Timothy. Their case, and their complaints against Jones' domination of his followers were taken up by Congressmen Leo Ryan, who eventually arranged a fact finding visit to the 'Jonestown' camp.

The visit did not go well, and when Ryan and his entourage left the camp for the nearby airstrip they invited any of Jones' followers to come back to America with them. Jones was convinced that they would be back with American or Guyanan troops to smash the commune. And, as they left, some of his followers panicked. On the way to the plane Ryan and three reporters were shot dead, and eight others were wounded. The plane eventually took off but while in the air, hardcore Jones follower Larry Layton produced a gun, shooting two passengers before being disarmed and jumping out.

In Jones' eyes the system had come to destroy his Masada, his fortified Garden of Eden. It was all over, and he knew just what to do.

Jones instigated his terminal policy, code-named 'White Night'. As his followers drank a lethal cocktail of cyanide, strawberry cola and tranquillisers, the Reverend spoke to this, his final congregation. His last words were recorded on a cassette by person or persons unknown and filed by the U.S. Government. The tape has been leaked, and now, with the co-operation of the World Surrealist Network, we can reproduce the complete transcript of these previously confidential last words. As document. As memorial. As insight.

Mad Jones and his sad followers were certainly not 'evil' people. They would have argued that they were not even misguided people. In a world of hypocrisy, of rampant materialism, of complacency and suppression. In a world of lies, Jones hurt by telling his confused truth.

The word 'suicide' usually conjures visions of hopelessness, helplessness, submission. Indeed, all these things are true in the case of Jonestown. But the Guyanan tragedy throws up something else. An element which – if we face it – is a part of each and every suicide. A failure on the part of Society. A failure to cope with individuals and groups who are dissatisfied. A failure to accommodate change, and embrace those people who see the world differently. A failure to love.

Something big was missing from the lives of those who volunteered for the Temple. And for all his egomania, his warped vision, his bullying and murder, Jones was really totally logical in his paranoid search for the truth. The result of his equation in this intolerant world of lies was inevitable: Death.

Indeed, this was a suicide. A revolutionary suicide.

[TAPE TRANSCRIPT STARTS]
[JIM JONES:] *"How very much I've tried my best to give you a good life. In spite of all that I've tried, a handful of people, with their lies, have made our lives impossible. There's no way to distract ourselves from what's happened today.*

"Not only do we have a compound situation, not only are there those who have left it to me [?] ...The Betrayal of the Century... Some have stolen children from mothers and are in pursuit right now to kill them, because they stole their children. I mean we are sitting here waiting on a powder-keg and I don't think that is what we want to do with our babies, I don't think that is what we have in mind to do with our babies.

"It was said by the greatest of prophets from time immemorial: `No man may take my life from me, I lay my life down...' So just to sit here and wait for the catastrophe that's going to happen on that airplane – It's going to be a catastrophe – It almost happened here, it almost happened, the congress-man was nearly killed here, but you can't steal people's children, you can't take off with people's children without expecting a violent reaction.

"And that's not so unfamiliar to us either, if we only look at the old Christians [?] who weren't communists...

"World opinion – violence, and violence – force. [?] But if we can't live in peace, then let us die in peace. I've been so betrayed. I've been so terribly betrayed. We've tried, and – what he said right this minute was that, he said if it was only worth one day it was worthwhile..."

[EDIT] *"Right then, what's going to happen in a few minutes is that one of the people on that plane is gonna, is gonna shoot the pilot, I know that. I didn't plan it but I know it's going to happen. They're gonna shoot that pilot and down comes the plane into the jungle and we had better not have any of our children left when it's over 'cause they'll – on us. The point is that this plane. I dunno how to say it... I've never lied to you, I never have lied to you.*

straight to hell

I know that's what's going to happen. That's what he intends to do and he will do it, he'll do it.

"What it means [?] I've been loaded with many pressures seeing all these people behave so treasonous. It was just too much for me to put together but I know what he was telling me and it'll happen... if the plane gets in the air that is.

"So my opinion is that you be kind to children and you be kind to seniors and take the potion like we used to take an ocean breeze and step over quietly because we are not committing suicide – it's a revolutionary act. We can't go back, we won't lose it for long [?] we're not going back to tell more lies which means more congressmen, there's no way, there's no way we can survive. Anyone that has any – opinion please speak".

[QUESTION FROM AUDIENCE]

"You'd be making a strike but we'd be making a strike against people we don't want to strike against. We'd like to get the people that caused this stuff and if some people are prepared and know how to do that tell it to Timothy Stone but there's no plane, there's no plane. We can't catch the plane in time".

[AUDIENCE]

[EDIT] *"He's [SHE'S?] responsible for it. He brought these people to us. He and Diana Myrtle. The people in San Francisco will not be idle over this. We do not take our death in vain you know."*

[AUDIENCE]

"Is it too late for Russia? Here's why it's too late for Russia. They killed, they started to kill. That's why it makes it too late for Russia. Otherwise I'd said – but it's too late. I can't control these people. They're out there. They've gone with the guns and it's too late. And once they've killed anybody, at least that's the way I want it. I just put my lot with you. If one of my people do something it's me. When they say I don't have to take the blame for this well I don't I don't live that way and if they deliver up – and try to get the man that's it. And – was – mother's being lying on him and lying on him and trying to break up this family and they've all agreed to kill us by whatever means necessary. Do you think I'm going to let them?... Not on your life. No you're not going, you're not going. You're not going. I can't live that way. I can not live that way. I've lived for all I'll die for all."

[EDIT] *"I've been living on hope for a long time, Christine, and I appreciate you've always been a good agitator and I like agitation because you have proof from two sides on one issue, on two sides of the question. And what those people going to get done, what they go through. They make our lives worse than hell. And make the rest of us not accept us. They tell so many lies there in that truck. We are not in as far as any alternative."*

[MORE QUESTIONS ABOUT RUSSIA FROM AUDIENCE]

"...but to me death is not a fearful thing, it's living that's fearful. I have never, never, never seen anything like this before in my life. I have never seen people take the law... and do – and provoke us and try to purposely agitate mothers of children.

"It is only... it's not, it's not worth living like this, worth living like this."

[TESTIMONIAL FROM AUDIENCE]

"There is one man there who blames, who blames Michael Stone for the murder of his mother, and he will stop that plane by any means necessary. He'll do it. That plane will come out of the air. There's no way you can fly a plane without a pilot..."

[MORE TALK ABOUT RUSSIA]

"I haven't seen anybody yet that didn't die, and I like to choose my own kind of death. I'm tired of being – to hell, that's what I'm tired of... Tired of it. So many people's lives in my hands and I certainly don't want your life in my hands. I've been telling you to this day, without me life has no meaning. I'm the best friend you'll ever have. I have to pay. I'm standing with you people – you're part of me. I can detach myself... I – detach myself, no, no, no, no, no, I never detach myself from any of your troubles. I've always taken your troubles right on my shoulders... I'm not going to change that now. It's too late. I've been running too long. I'm not gonna change now. The next time, you'll get to Russia. The next time round. This is... what I'm talking about now is the dispensation of judgement, this is a revolutionary suicide council. I'm not talking about self... self- destruction. I'm talking about what... we have no other road. I will take your call. I will put it to the Russians, and I can tell you the answer now because I'm a prophet. Call the Russians and tell them... see if they'll take us."

straight to hell

[AUDIENCE]

"I tried to give it to you (peace). I laid down my life practically. I practically died every day to give you peace. And you've still not had any peace. You look better than I've seen you in a long while, but it's still not the kind of peace that I wanted to give you.

"A person's a fool who continues to say that you're winning when you're losing. Win one, lose two, what?..."

[AUDIENCE]

"He's taking off, the plane is taking off... Suicide many have done it... Stone has done it. If somebody oughta lis... somebody... can they talk... can they not talk to San Francisco? See that Stone is not here by – the sins of men... He has done the thing he wanted to do. To have us destroyed."

[AUDIENCE]

"We win, we win when we go down, they don't have anybody else to hate. They've got nobody else to hate. Many will destroy themselves. I'm speaking here not as the administrator but as a prophet today. I wouldn't – talk serious if I didn't know what I was talking about.

"Has anybody called back... the men... by now the damage will be done. But I cannot separate myself from the pain of my people. We can't separate myself, if you think about it [?] we've walked together too long."

[AUDIENCE]

"I saved them, I saved them, but I made my example. I made my expression. I made my manifestation and the world was ready... not ready for me. Paul says I was a man born out of due season. I've been born out of due season just like all we are and the best testimony we can make is to leave this Goddam world."

[AUDIENCE]

"Everybody hold it, hold it, hold it... lay down your burden and I'll lay down my burden, down by the riverside, shall we lay 'em down here inside of Guyana, what's the difference? No man didn't take our lives right now he hasn't taken them, but when they start shooting them out of the air, they'll shoot some of our innocent babies. I'm not lying... it's fifty, there's fifty but they've gotta shoot me to get through to some of these people. I'm not letting them take your child. Would you let them take your child?"

[AUDIENCE]

"For months I've tried to keep this thing from happening, but I now see that it's the will of the Sovereign Being that this happened to us. And we lay down our lives in protest at what's been done. And we lay in protest to what's been done. The criminality of people, the cruelty of people, who walked out of here today. You know those people who walked out, most of those white people. Most of those white people walked. I'm so grateful for the ones that didn't, those who knew who they are. There's no point, there's no point to this... we have... we are born before our time.

"They won't accept us. And I don't think we should sit here and take any more time for our children to be endangered and if they come after our children and we give them our children, then our children will suffer forever.

"You have to be honest and if you say that you want to run you'd have run with them 'cause anybody could have run today... I know you are not a runner and I'd... your life is precious to me – it's as precious as John's [?] I don't... what I do I do with weight [?] and justice and judgement. And I have waited against all evidence... Take ease, take ease, take ease, take ease, take ease... Sit down sit down sit down. I tried so very very hard... what's gonna happen... who is it? Get Dwyer out of here before something happens to him."

[AUDIENCE]

"It's all over, it's all over... What a legacy, what a legacy well the Red Brigade's the only ones that made any sense anyway. They invaded our privacy, they invaded our home, they followed us six thousand miles away. The Red Brigade showed them justice – the congressman's dead.

"Please get some medication... it's simple, there's no convulsions with it. It's just simple. Please get it before it's too late. The GDF will be here I tell you. Get moving, get moving, get moving. Don't be afraid to die. If these people land out here they'll torture our children, they'll torture some of our people here, they'll torture our seniors. We cannot have this. Are you going to separate yourself from whoever shot the congressman. I don't know who shot him. They speak of peace, they gotta right to how many are dead... Oh God, Almighty God..."

[AUDIENCE]

straight to hell

"I don't know how in the world they are ever gonna write about us. It's too late, it's too late. The congressman is dead. The congresslady's [?] dead... many of our traitors are dead... They're all laying out there dead."

[AUDIENCE]

"I didn't but my people did. They're my people and they've been provoked too much. They've been provoked too much. What's happened here has been too... has been an act of provocation."

[AUDIENCE]

"Will you please hasten, will you hasten with that medication. You don't know what you've done... I've tried... They saw it happen, ran into the bush and dropped the machine guns... You've got to move, you've got to get that medication, you've got to move. Might be in about 20 minutes."

[MEMBER OF AUDIENCE, NOT J.J.:]

'One of the things I used to do before I came here, was I used to be a therapist. It might make a lot of you more comfortable. Sit down & be quiet please. One of the things I used to do, I used to be a therapist and the kind of therapy that I did had to do with reincarnation and past lives... Everybody was so happy when they stepped through to the other side...'

[J.J.:] "You've gotta step that way. It's the only way to step. The choice is not ours now, it's out of our hands..."

[AUDIENCE]

"And I do hope that those battalions will stay where they belong and don't come up here..."

[AUDIENCE]

"It's hard, it's hard only at first is it hard. It's hard only at first. Living... when you're looking at death... it only looks... living is much more difficult... Raising up every morning and not knowing what's going to be... the night brings... it's much more difficult. It's much more difficult...

"No, no sorrow that it's all over. I'm glad it's over. Hurry, hurry my children hurry... let us not fall in the hands of the enemy. Hurry my children, hurry. There are seniors out here that I'm concerned about, hurry. I don't want to leave my seniors to this mess. Now quickly, quickly, quickly, quickly, quickly... No more pain Al. No more pain I said Al. No more pain. Jim Cobb is laying on the airfield dead at this moment. Remember the moment... all of the

56

moments that he... These are the people, the pedlars of hate.

"All we're doing is laying down our life, we're not letting them take our life, we're laying down our life. We're sick of their lies, we just want peace."

[TESTIMONIAL FROM AUDIENCE]

"All it is is taking a drink to take... to go to sleep. That's what death is, sleep. [SCREAMS] Whatever, I'm tired of it all."

[TESTIMONIAL FROM AUDIENCE]

"If you don't... don't fail to follow my advice you'll be sorry. You'll be sorry... If we do it then let they do it. Have trust in... you have to step across. We used to sing. This world, this world it's not our home, well it sure isn't. We were saying, it sure wasn't. And we don't want to tell him... the only thing [?] to tell him... assure these kids, can some people assure these children of the relaxation of stepping over to the next plane. We'll set an example for others... we set... one thousand people who've said we don't like the way the world is.

"Free at last... Keep... keep your emotions down, keep your emotions down... The – will not hurt if you will keep your emotions down, if you will be quiet. [SCREAMS] It's never been done before you say?... It's been done by every tribe in history. Every tribe facing annihilation... All the Indians of the Amazon are doing it right now. They refuse to bring any babies in the world. They kill every child that comes into the world, because they don't want to live in this kind of world. Be patient, be patient. Death is...

"I tell you I don't care how many screams you hear. I don't care how many anguished cries... Death is a million times preferable to ten more days of this life. If you knew what was ahead of you, if you knew what was ahead of you you'd be glad to be stepping over tonight. Death, death, death is common to people. If you ask the Samoans they take death in their stride... Just have dignity, just be dignified... If you'll quit tell 'em they're dying... If you adults will stop some of this nonsense... Adults, adults, adults, I call on you to stop this nonsense... I call on you to quit exciting your children when all they're doing is going to quiet rest. I call on you to stop this now if you have any respect at all. Are we black, proud and socialist or what are we? Now stop this nonsense. Don't carry this on any more. You're exciting your children."

[AUDIENCE]

Straight to hell

"Please for God's sake let's get on with it. We've lived as no other people have lived and loved. We've had as much of this world as you're gonna get. Let's just be done with it, let's be done with the agony of it. It's far, far harder to have to watch you every day die slowly, and from the time you're a child to the time you get grey, you are dying... dishonest and I'm sure that they'll pay for it... This is a revolutionary suicide. It's not a self-destructive suicide. They'll pay for this. They brought this upon us, and they'll pay for that – I leave that destiny to them. [SCREAMS] Who wants to go with their child has a right to go with their child I think it's humane. I want to go – I want to see you go though. They can take me, and they can do whatever they want to do. I want to see you go. I don't wanna see you go through this hell no more. No more, no more, no more, we're trying... somebody relax... the best thing you can do is relax and you will have no problem. You will have no problem with the thing if you just relax."

[TESTIMONIALS FROM AUDIENCE]

"It's not to be feared. It is not to be feared. It's a friend. As you're sitting there show your love for one another..."

First published in *Rapid Eye 1* (Creation Books, 1995)

kurt cobain

The history of rock and roll is littered with the corpses of musicians consumed by their own passion, angst, and nasty habits. From Hendrix choking to death on his own vomit to Elvis lying bloated on the marble floor of his Graceland bathroom, all the greatest rock heroes and heroines come to a sorry end. Just think of Janis Joplin, overdosing on whisky and speedballs at the Franklin Avenue motel in Hollywood; think of Jim Morrison lying bloated in his Paris bathtub; think of Michael Hutchence hanging from the door of his room at the Ritz Carlton in Sydney.

Many of these accidents and overdoses may have been driven by unconscious motivations to suicide, but rock stars who deliberately take their own lives – especially when at the height of their success – are less common than the popular imagination likes to believe. On April 8 1994, the body of Kurt Cobain, lead singer with the Seattle grunge band Nirvana, was found dead of a shotgun wound to the head. The gun with which Cobain shot himself – a 20-gauge Remington M11 semi-automatic shotgun – was actually purchased not by Kurt, but by his best friend, Dylan Carlson, on March 20 1994. Cobain wanted the gun for self-protection, and asked Dylan to purchase it under his name so it couldn't be confiscated by the police – the fate of several other weapons removed from Kurt's home during a "domestic disturbance."

For those who decide on suicide by firearm, the shotgun is certainly the way to go. Shotguns are easy to obtain – in the U.S., at least – and death is usually instantaneous. As with most suicide methods, however, there is a slim chance of survival; the occasional case is reported in which the would-be suicide misses their brain entirely, just blowing off their face instead. Another drawback of the shotgun suicide is that it can be amazingly messy, leaving loved ones the sorry task of cleaning festering lumps of gore out of the carpet.

Cobain's suicide was apparently fairly neat; the grunge guru killed himself by placing the barrel of the shotgun against the upper palate of his mouth, which absorbed much of the blast; the shot remained inside Cobain's skull, and most of his head remained intact. His corpse was discovered in the greenhouse of his Seattle by a contractor who arrived to complete some electrical work, and who immediately informed the police.

A well-publicized suicide note was found beside Cobain's body, part of which was read to crowds of mourning fans by Kurt's wife, Courtney Love, at the Lollapalooza festival in summer 1994. "This note should be pretty easy to understand," wrote Cobain. "All the warnings from the Punk Rock 101 corpses over the years since my first introduction to the, shall we say, ethics involved with independence and embracement of your community, it's proven to be very true. I haven't felt the excitement of listening to as well as creating music, along with really writing something, for too many years now. I feel guilty beyond words for these things. For example, when we're backstage and the lights go out and the roar of the crowd begins, it doesn't affect me the way in which it did for Freddy Mercury, who seemed to love and relish the love and adoration of the crowd, which is something I totally admire and envy. The fact that I can't fool you, any one of you, it simply isn't fair to you or me. The worst crime I could think of would be to pull people off by faking it, pretending as if I'm having one hundred percent fun."

This letter seems to have been intended not so much for the police or for Courtney Love as for Cobain's many adoring fans, explaining his untimely departure from the music maelstrom. The tone of the note suggests that it was written to explain Kurt's suicide to the public, hence his widow's decision to read it out loud to his fans at Lollapalooza. In an interview with *Rolling Stone* magazine, Courtney Love also mentioned the existence of a second note, which Kurt had written directly to her, and which she decided not to make public.

Kurt Cobain had apparently been suicidal for a long time prior to his death. Apart from the existential angst he describes in his note, Cobain had been unable to kick a lifetime addiction to heroin – his works were found on the floor lying beside his dead body, and, according to police reports, he'd given himself a fix in both arms only minutes before his death. He'd recently walked out on a $9.5 million contract, attempted suicide in an Italian hotel room, and, less than a week before his death, entered rehab in Marina del Ray, California – which he quit the following day.

The suicide of a prominent youth icon is often followed by outbreaks of suicide by depressed and empathetic fans. This phenomenon is sometimes referred to as the "Werther syndrome," and was first witnessed in modern culture with the death of Rudolph Valentino, which sparked an epidemic of empathy suicides. In the days and weeks following the death of Kurt Cobain, a rash of fans from Seattle to Australia began killing themselves in empathy and tribute to the fallen grunge king.

Seattle police classed Cobain's death as a suicide, and yet – as with all similar cases – alternative theories about Cobain's death are widespread, most of them fingering rock widow Courtney Love as the suspect with the most to gain out of her husband's death. Even before Cobain's death, many fans of Nirvana already thought Courtney Love, with her notorious ambition and fierce temper, was a dark influence on Cobain and the band. Three months before his death, Cobain allegedly told a reporter from *Rolling Stone* that he might be divorcing Courtney in the near future. After his death, the magazine reported that divorce papers were already being drawn up at the time of Cobain's suicide.

straight to hell

Those who believe in the conspiracy have claimed that Kurt and Courtney were on the verge of vicious divorce proceedings, and Kurt had instructed lawyers to remove Courtney from his will. And they also claim that Courtney had a lot to gain from her husband's suicide: Nirvana records would skyrocket in popularity, and Courtney's band Hole would win extra publicity into the bargain. Both of these events occurred immediately after Cobain's death, in fact, when Nirvana's "Unplugged in New York" debuted at the top of the charts, and Hole ended up taking the place of Nirvana at Lollapalooza 1994. Ironically, Lollapaloooza was the $9.5 million dollar deal Cobain had walked out of shortly before his death.

Seattle-based conspiracy researcher Richard Lee, host of the cable access show "Kurt Cobain was Murdered," believes that Courtney Love blamed Kurt's walking out on the Lollapalooza deal on his drug use, and arranged a "tough love" intervention involving some of his junkie friends. When this failed, and when Cobain quit rehab after only one day, Love apparently hired a private detective to find out who was using a credit card belonging to Cobain which she had personally cut into pieces. Apparently, the charges on the credit card continued beyond the time of Kurt's death, but stopped abruptly just before his body was discovered.

According to Richard Lee, on Monday April 4, somebody claiming to be Kurt's mother called the Seattle police department with a missing person's report. Police records say that this person claimed "Mr. Cobain ran away from CA facility and flew back to Seattle. He also bought a shotgun and may be suicidal." Lee believes that the call was actually placed by Courtney Love, who later called her private detective and told him that "Everybody thinks Kurt's going to die."

If Cobain's death did involve foul play, however, the police must have also been involved in the cover-up, as well as the media which reported information handed out by police, reinforcing the official findings of suicide. Still, conspiracy or not, it seems clear that Cobain was, like many great artists, a deeply suicidal personality. Stories about cover-ups and other skullduggery are, in the case of Kurt Cobain, perhaps not unexpected. His death made him into a rock legend, and the story of his death has the feeling of a wider tragedy.

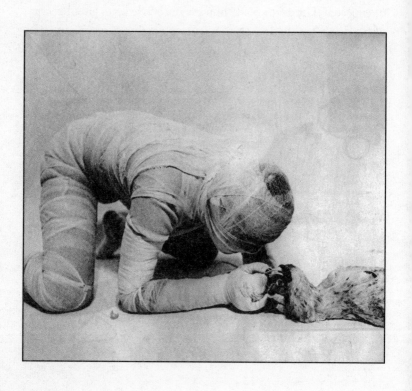

rudolf Schwarzkogler

In the white-hot arena of mid-1960s experimental performance art, the most haunting and compelling images are those that document the work of an Austrian artist, Rudolf Schwarzkogler, then in his mid-twenties, who created actions in which enigmatic human figures swathed entirely in medical bandages undergo extreme acts of sexual attack that reveal the acute vulnerability and isolation of physical matter: male sexual organs are supplanted by fish-flesh and razor-blades, the hidden body and face are painfully entangled in a wasteland of wire, metal implements and illuminated lightbulbs, and an aura of infinite danger and negation hangs over the human body. Schwarzkogler undertook his performance works almost covertly, staging his actions with a few friends and documenting them solely through photography. While allying himself with the legendary participants of the Vienna Action Group – Hermann Nitsch, with his eviscerated and crucified animal carcasses deluged in blood, Otto Muehl, with his hard-core orgiastic sexual performances of sodomy and social refusal, and Gunther Brus, with his scandalous public defecations and razor-blade self-mutilations – Schwarzkogler remained in isolation, rarely appearing publicly and incessantly interrogating the ultimate meaning of his work. While Nitsch, Muehl and Brus delighted in actively provoking and outraging the stultified citizens of Vienna (incurring accumulating fines and prison sentences for their 'art-crimes'), performing in public venues or in the streets of Vienna,

Schwarzkogler turned more and more into himself.

Like most of the participants of the Vienna Action Group, Schwarzkogler was deeply marked by the Second World War. He was the youngest of the Group, having been born in 1940. The oldest participant of the Action Group, Otto Muehl, was fifteen years older and had served as a young soldier in the Nazi army in the last desperate days of the war; Muehl had regularly seen his young comrades eviscerated, decapitated and blown to smoking fragments of liquefied flesh-pulp as they retreated headlong in front of the unstoppable advance of Stalin's communism-powered army, as it relentlessly advanced on Vienna, summarily massacring or raping everything in sight. Schwarzkogler's own father had been a Nazi doctor on the eastern front and had been present at the Battle of Stalingrad, where the entire course of the Second World War abruptly pivoted from Hitler's apparently-imminent worldwide victory to the onset of his defeat. The endless Stalingrad casualties formed mountains of human meat in the shattered city and the surrounding battlefields. On 13 January 1943, Schwarzkogler's father had his legs blown off in an explosion during the battle and, in agony, promptly blew his own head off with a blast of machine-gun fire; only the trunk and arms were left to be hastily buried, along with the millions of other battle-casualties. His son Rudolf, back in Austria, was two years old at the time. By the moment that the Soviet army finally reached Vienna, just over two years later, that city too was in bombed-out ruins, its surviving population ripe for a week-long bout of wholesale anal-rape and slaughter at the hands of the revenge-impelled totalitarian hordes of Stalin.

By the mid-1960s, Schwarzkogler had abandoned art school and was spending his time assiduously reading Artaud and Bataille. All of his six performance actions were staged in 1965 and 1966, either in his own apartment or in that of his friend Heinz Cibulka, who usually served as the 'model' of the bandaged figure in Schwarzkogler's actions; Schwarzkogler was intensely self-critical, and only the final one of those six actions gave him any satisfaction. His imageries of immobilised human figures, their penises bandaged and surrounded by scissors, their mouths trailing wire, were conceived explicitly for the photographic documents which remain their sole evidence. He also occasionally participated in the work of the other Action Group artists – notably serving as a model for Nitsch's infamous 'penis-rinsing' actions of the mid-1960s, and can also be seen in the film and photographic documentation of Brus's 'Vienna Walk' action, in which Brus (painted white, with a line separating his body in two) strode through the central areas of Vienna, notably in front of the palace balcony from which Hitler had announced the annexation of Austria to ecstatic crowds in 1938. Schwarzkogler never attempted to make any money from his art, and worked during the day as a graphic designer for most of the time he was involved with the Action Group.

After staging his sixth action in Spring 1966 (in which he served as his own model), Schwarzkogler retreated still further into his solitary obsessions. During the subsequent three years, the other three Action Group artists intensified their reputation for scandal and became the subject of media-frenzies in Austria and across Europe. After a spectacular performance of public defecation on 7 June 1968 – during which he energetically masturbated while singing the Austrian national anthem – Brus received a two-year prison sentence and had to flee to Berlin; Nitsch and Muehl were also pursued and vilified as they tried to stage their spectacles of blood and semen-drenched slaughter (Nitsch finally acquired a derelict castle to the north of Vienna and staged his actions there in seclusion, while Muehl founded a nihilistic free-sex farm-commune to the south-east of Vienna before being imprisoned during the 1990s for child-sex). In his isolation, Schwarzkogler increasingly experimented with starvation techniques inspired by dietary prohibitions, until his body grew skeletal, weak and exhausted, and he spent his time contemplating the void.

On 20 June 1969, Schwarzkogler reached the final point of those contemplations. On the previous day, he had visited a therapist with his friend Heinz Cibulka, and had been told that he would need electroshock treatment to launch him back into the world. Instead, Schwarzkogler chose another strategy of self-launching. In the previous month, he had moved to an apartment directly alongside the main Vienna market, at 20 Heumühlgasse, where the other tenants had already become deeply suspicious of their Actionist neighbour (by this time, Schwarzkogler was the last of the Action Group remaining in Vienna – the others had all fled or gone into exile). On the morning of that day, Schwarzkogler leapt from the window of his third-floor apartment, landing on his back on the pavement below. A crowd of his neighbours and some interested passers-by soon gathered as the artist convulsed and muttered in agony – his back broken but otherwise unscathed – and began to berate him for what they assumed to be another piece of abject public art-scandal. After a few minutes of jerking spasms and remonstrations, Schwarzkogler suffered what his autopsy described as a 'fat embolism' – the shattered pieces of spinal marrow blocked the arterial passage of blood into his heart – and expired. In later years, as his legend grew, many stories would be invented about his death (the addled Australian journalist Robert Hughes claimed Schwarzkogler had sliced off his own penis during a performance), but Schwarzkogler had expertly chosen his own distinctive means of soaring exit from what he viewed as an accursed, wounded and terminally banal world.

gilles deleuze

I Corpus Delicti

"Let's pretend there's a way of getting through into it, somehow, Kitty. Let's pretend the glass has got all soft like gauze, so that we can get through. Why, it's turning into a sort of mist now, I declare! It'll be easy enough to get through–' She was up on the chimney-piece while she said this, though she hardly knew how she had got there. And certainly the glass WAS beginning to melt away, just like a bright silvery mist."[1]

Saturday 4th November 1995: On Niel Avenue in the 17th arrondissement of Paris, several people may have gathered, there may have even been quite a crowd. Before them, the body of philosopher Gilles René Louis Deleuze. After his body having become increasingly consolidated, after an operation to remove one of his lungs, after a tracheotomy, but before the prospect of institutionalisation became concrete, Deleuze took to a window and jumped.

So what to make of it? When writers expire, there are always attempts to correlate the circumstances of death within the newly established corpus.[2] Deleuze's suicide led more than a few to jump to conclusions that equally articulated their inability to conceptualise the event outside of philosophy…

"I didn't really read that closely all of the postings from these last two days because they all seemed to be "Oh please tell me that bitch is lying", "How will we talk about his death?", "Let us talk about his death correctly", "We are reducing his texts to platitudes", " I know better than you how to talk about his death", etc... Deleuze jumped out of a window and it must have been horrible and wonderful, or perhaps the most banal footnote in all of history. A body goes thump and some miserable concierge pulls out a bucket to clean it up."[3]

...And there were, as one might expect, a series of speculations about the event via concepts created by Deleuze (& Guattari) that seemed appropriate to those attempting to come to terms with the news:

"...But hurling from a window - rich, appropriate - a last line of flight? ...the day I found about all this (Tuesday), I had been working on "La logique de la sensation" and one of the chapters (number X) deals with "la chute", the fall... The pavement is no concern of Deleuze's, of course. But as a matter of fact, it is a concern of ours – a matter of concrete substance, and expressive of a surface of contact with Deleuze's body. Pavement leaps, pavement shudders, pavement becomes delirious, see? ...reading Deleuze's suicide does not negate or overshadow his philosophy; it illuminates the philosophy."[4]

Taking recourse to the corpus of Deleuze in order to make sense of the suicide reinforces the rigid demarcation of the corpus further narrowing it to moments in the work that linguistically relate to the event; lines of flight, la chute, not to mention the actual occurrences of suicide and death in the texts. But this is a dogged path that runs contrary to the way in which Deleuze thought and wrote. These pickings, temporarily tasty as they may be, unwittingly convert Deleuze's work into a totality, a corpus vile: something felt to be of so little value that it may be experimented with or upon without concern for loss or damage. In the rush to locate a reason, a meaning, and consequently a truth; the truth of the event, Deleuze is turned against his own work and both are turned towards each other; linked in an inseparable pairing.

II **Corpus Striatum**

"The philosophies that promise to teach us what to think about death and how to die bore me to tears. I'm not at all moved by those things that are supposed to 'prepare us for it.' One has to prepare it bit by bit, decorate it, arrange the details, find the ingredients, imagine it, choose it, get advice on it, shave it into a work without spectators, one which exists only for oneself, just for that shortest little moment of life. Those who survive, of course, see suicide as nothing but superficial traces, solitude, awkwardness, and unanswered cries. These people can't help but ask 'why?' the only question about death that shouldn't be asked."[5]

It's hardly difficult to locate utter refutations of asking *why?* in Deleuze's (& Guattari's) work;

"...we will not look for anything to understand in it. We will ask what it functions with, in connection with what other things it does or does not transmit intensities, in which other multiplicities its own are inserted and metamorphosed, and with what bodies without organs it makes its own converge."[6]

Despite the obvious pitfalls, other, more well-known figures also turned to Deleuze's work for an appropriate marker; a locale from which to consider again the question of the act and what it means for us, as opposed to finding something to traverse the boundary of the corpus: Jacques Derrida's tribute[7] traces through Deleuze's work to locate a suitable quote for 'the thinker of the event' and arrives at " 'We are faced with a volitional intuition and a

straight to hell

transmutation. To my inclination for death' said Bousquet, 'which was a failure of the will, I will substitute a longing for death, which is the apotheosis of the will.' from this inclination to this longing there is, in a certain respect, no change except a change of the will, a sort of leaping in place (*saut sur place*) of the whole body which exchanges its organic will for a spiritual will."[8]

It's tempting to again focus on the leap, the paradoxical 'leaping in place' that provides Derrida with the kind of figure he can write through and yet another reference to jumping for us, but it is the Will which is pursued through the quotation; the flux of becoming and passing away is not passive but an active process

"It is highly probable that resignation is only one more figure of *ressentiment*, since *ressentiment* has many figures. If willing the event is, primarily, to release its eternal truth, like the fire on which it is fed, this will would reach the point at which war is waged against war, the wound would be the living trace and the scar of all wounds, and death turned on itself would be willed against all deaths."[9]

In turning to Deleuze's philosophy, to his references to death and/or suicide, we enter a debate in which it is always the will in relation to death that is at stake. In the Phaedo, Plato suggests that "…there may be reason in saying that a man should wait, and not take his own life until God summons him…"[10]

Deleuze's suicide re-articulates his opposition to the "court of Pure Reason"[11] and without much effort we can trace a history of the conceptualisation of suicide counter to the court: "Above all, remember that the door stands open. Do not be more fearful than children. But, just as when they are tired if the game they cry, "I will play no more," so too when you are in a similar situation, cry "I will play no more" and depart. But if you stay, do not cry"[12]

As we turn towards the corpus and then to related

philosophical precedents, we face the problematics of turning towards a "Greek image of thought" which "already invoked the madness of the double turning-away" and "which launched thought into infinite wandering":[13]

"I will not relinquish my old age if it leaves my better part intact. But if it begins to shake my mind, if it destroys my faculties one by one, if it leaves me not life but breath, I will depart from the putrid or the tottering edifice. If I know that I must suffer without hope of relief I will depart not through fear of the pain itself but because it prevents all for which I should live."[14]

Reading this quote from Seneca, the connections to the circumstances of Deleuze's suicide are brought sharply into focus, but they serve to obscure Seneca's point rather than illuminate Deleuze's act. It is the undeniable locating of the eye on correlative information that leads us both towards and away from the event. So should we continue to wander along these distinct trails in Deleuze's works and their bibliographies? Should we pursue the investigation along Deleuze's lines?

As Deleuze (and Guattari) always maintained "...make a map, not a tracing... a map has multiple entryways, as opposed to the tracing, which always comes back 'to the same.' The map has to do with performance, whereas the tracing always involves an alleged 'competence.' "[15] This pursuit still runs conversely to the question we have posed; what to make of it? If we continue to trace Deleuze's steps, if we follow behind him, if we jump out of the window after him, can we make anything of it at all?

III Corpus Vile II

"All this time the Guard was looking at her, first through a telescope, then through a microscope, and then through an opera-glass. At last he said, 'You're travelling the wrong way,' and shut

straight to hell

up the window and went away."[16]

Little trips, endless indices, pick ups, archives, borrowings; defenestres, suidas, fell odyssey, Windows 95, Lao Tsu, Mary Poppins, Yves Klein, Hitchcock, Post-mortemism, scratched vinyl, fingernails, bolt holes, doctores angelici, go, Hradcany, Gardyloo, Rezso Seress.

In a series of filmed interviews,[17] intended for broadcast after his death, Deleuze speaks of "un bon coin pour mourir."[18] I won't continue to attempt to detect what constitutes this corner, elaborate on its demarcations, tie up all of the loose ends like the model detective, who "...in the end always prefers a handful of "certainty" to a whole cartload of beautiful possibilities"[19]

IV Corpus Exterus

Outside of the institution, away from academic proofing, Deleuze's philosophy continues through people literally taking up the conception of philosophy as always needing to be opened up to an outside, of concepts to be created and as tools to be used; "...people are constantly putting up an umbrella that shelters them and on the underside of which they draw a firmament and write their conventions and opinions. But poets, artists, make a slit in the umbrella, they tear open the firmament itself, to let in a bit of free and windy chaos and to frame in a sudden light a vision that appears through the rent..."[20]

The release of 'Folds & Rhizomes: In Memoriam Gilles Deleuze' on Sub Rosa in February 1996 still serves to remind us that Deleuze's work was not ever entirely the province of the academic community;

"...it seems to us that living in his memory as a school is a disaster to be avoided at all costs. And anyone who acts - in no matter what field – using his concepts as tools, will be closer to him than any academic self – proclaiming himself to be Deleuzian…"[21] Like many obituaries, the works on the compilation had been produced before Deleuze's death, not in anticipation of it; "I said to myself, …there is no better way to be in Deleuze than to use the philosophy and draw a tangent towards something else… I learned of his death on the radio. Something in me said: too late. But the testimonial is still there. Indeed it wasn't a tribute, the whole thing was conceived in life."[22]

Postscript

"I found a Liberation hanging out of a trash can. It smelled like someone's lunch… Some guy I don't know reported that Deleuze used to tell him something like, "C'est ton chagrin idiot…." Enfin."[23]

[1] Lewis Carroll, *Through the Looking Glass.* Penguin (1998)

[2] Notably Italo Calvino's '*In memory of Roland Barthes*', *The Literature Machine*, Verso (1997)

[3] post to the deleuze-guattari list in the week following the news: http://lists.village.virginia.edu/cgi-bin/spoons/archive1.pl?list=deleuze-guattari.archive/d-g_1995/d-g_Nov.95

[4] Ibid; deleuze.guattari list

[5] Michel Foucault in *Foucault Live: Collected Interviews, 1961-1984* Sylvère Lotringer (Ed) SEMIOTEXT(E). New York. (1996) p295

[6] G. Deleuze & F. Guattari, *A Thousand Plateaus.* Athlone Press (1988) p4

[7] Jacques Derrida, *I Shall Have to Wander all Alone* in *The Work of Mourning.* Univ. Chicago Press (2001)

[8] Gilles Deleuze, *The Logic of Sense.* Athlone Press, (1990) p149

[9] ibid. p149

[10] Plato, *Phaedo,* Prometheus Books (1994) p62

[11] Gilles Deleuze, *Dialogues.* Columbia University Press (1989) p9

[12] Epictectus , *The Golden Sayings of Epictectus*, XLIV

[13] G. Deleuze & F. Guattari, *What is Philosophy.* (Verso 1994) p54

[14] Seneca, *De Ira*, 1:15

[15] G. Deleuze & F. Guattari, *A Thousand Plateaus.* Athlone Press (1988) p12/13

[16] Lewis Carroll, *Through the Looking Glass.* Penguin ()

[17] Pierre-André Boutang [dir.], *L'Abécédaire de Gilles Deleuze, avec Claire Parnet,* (1996)

[18] "A good corner(or place) to die"

[19] F. Nietszche, *Beyond Good and Evil,* Penguin (1990) p10

[20] G. Deleuze & F. Guattari, *What is Philosophy.* Verso (1994) p203

[21] **DOUBLE ARTICULATION**: ANOTHER PLATEAU, liner notes, Sub Rosa (1997)

[22] Ibid.

[23] Douglas Edric, Paris. 8.11.1995

fred west

Fred West may not have been England's most charismatic mass murderer, but few other criminals have led lives of such constant violence and moral vacuity. Born in 1941 in the village of Much Marcle, approximately 120 miles west of London, Frederick West was the oldest son of Walter and Daisy West, who came from a long line of Herefordshire farm laborers. Despite their poverty, the Wests went on to have six more children after Fred, all within the space of ten years. Surprisingly, his childhood sees to have been a happy one; he was especially close to his mother, and admired his father as a role model. He claims that his father had sex with his daughters and that he himself got one of his sisters pregnant, but since West proved such a notorious liar, these allegations have been difficult to prove.

Fred grew into an unattractive and unpromising child; his hair was always wild and unkempt, his mouth was too big and he had a gap between his two front teeth. At school, he was constantly in trouble and always getting caned. He left school at fifteen, almost illiterate, and went to work as a farm hand. At the age of seventeen he was seriously injured in a motorcycle accident which left him in a coma for a week, and with a metal plate in his head. Some believe this injury made him prone to sudden fits of rage that may have played a significant part in his criminal history.

Always sexually aggressive, at seventeen Fred was arrested for impregnating a 13-year-old girl; he got off without a jail sentence, but became distanced from his family. As a result, he left home and began to lead a transient life, stealing from construction sites and having sex with young girls whenever he could get away with it. In November 1962, he married Rena Costello, a teenage delinquent with a record of prostitution and burglary who was, at the time she married Fred, pregnant by an Asian bus driver. In March 1963 Rena gave birth to a daughter, Charmaine, and in 1964 she bore a child by Fred, who was named Anne Marie. Around this time, Fred met a girl named Anna McFall, whose boyfriend had been killed in an accident, and invited her to move in with himself and Rene in a *menage à trois*.

West supported his family by taking a series of odd jobs; in 1965, however, he was offered permanent work in a Gloucester slaughterhouse, and he and his family moved into a trailer in the town. It has been speculated that this job in the slaughterhouse had a profound effect on Fred; he seems to have developed a morbid obsession with corpses, blood and dismemberment. He also had a voracious and aggressive sexual appetite, demanding oral sex, bondage and sodomy at all hours of the day and night. Significantly, as soon as Fred West moved to Gloucester, a number of sexual assaults began to be reported in the area, many of them committed by a man of Fred's description.

In early 1967, Anna McFall became pregnant with Fred's child, and began attempting to persuade Fred to divorce Rena and marry her. Instead, Fred murdered Anna, dismembered her corpse and buried her near their trailer some time in July. Oddly enough, he also cut off her fingers and toes, which were never recovered—something that would become his ritualistic signature in later crimes. After killing Anna, he sent Rena out to earn money as a prostitute, while he remained at home molesting his two infant daughters. After a series of disagreements between the couple, Rena temporarily returned home to Scotland, and it was at this time, in November 1968, that Fred met the woman who would become his lifelong partner in crime, Rose Letts. At the age of sixteen, while Fred was in prison for various petty thefts, Rose

Letts moved into the house he was renting on Midland Road to take care of Charmaine and Anna Marie.

In 1970, Rose gave birth to a daughter, Heather, and in 1971 either Fred, Rose or the pair of them was responsible for the death of Charmaine, who was killed—her fingers and toes removed—and buried under the floor of the kitchen at Midland Road. By this time Fred had married Rose, so when his first wife Rena returned from Scotland to claim her child, there was only one option open. Rena's remains were buried under the house at Midland Road, alongside those of her daughter.

Over the next twenty-five years, Fred and Rose West embarked upon a sordid life of murder, incest and prostitution, burying a series of dismembered bodies in the back garden of the house they bought together at 25 Cromwell Street, Gloucester – later christened by the media as the "House of Horrors." The inside of the house was large and had a garage and a sizable cellar, which Fred, who loved gadgets, soundproofed and made into a torture chamber where he would strap down and rape and beat his daughters and other women he abducted.

Gloucester had a large population of West Indians, and Rose would often invite them over to have sex with her, sometimes for money, sometimes just for fun. Fred would watch through a peephole, sometimes taking photographs of the proceedings. He set his wife up as a prostitute, running photos of her as ads in magazines for swingers. "Normal" sex was of no interest to Fred; he sought out the perverse and peculiar, and filled his torture chamber with bondage equipment, vibrators, handcuffs and chains.

Some of Fred's victims were homeless young girls or runaways who came to stay at Cromwell Street at the Wests invitation; others were abducted from the street or the bus stop. No-one knows how many people Fred West murdered, in total, although one of his victims was certainly his daughter Heather, who was killed when she was sixteen, and buried under the patio.

Other known victims include eighteen-year-old Linda Gough, fifteen-year-old Carol Ann Cooper, twenty-one-year-old Therese Siegenthaler, fifteen-year-old Shirley Lloyd, eighteen-year-old Juanita Mott, twenty-one-year-old Lucy Partington, and sixteen-year-old Alison Chambers. The remains of seven bodies were found buried at 25 Cromwell Street, most in the back garden, but some inside the floorboards of the house. West was considered guilty of at least twelve murders, but is believed to be responsible for many more. Rose West remains in prison for her involvement in the case, but continuously claims to have known nothing about her husband's dreadful crimes.

Fred West was not considered a suicide risk at Pucklechurch prison in Gloucestershire because of his relentlessly cheerful demeanour. In fact, he spent the morning of his suicide playing pool with his fellow prisoners. Nevertheless, he was accompanied by two guards at all times, and it was rare that he was alone for very long. One of these occasions was the lunch hour, when prison staff were changing shifts and taking their own breaks. After the guards had left him at 12 noon on New Year's Day of 1995, West stripped his bed sheets to make two ligatures and looped them around a small air vent above the door of his cell. From this, he hanged himself, his body preventing the door from being opened rapidly.

Although West's suicide came as a surprise, it fits the common pattern of inmate suicide. Prison inmates are more likely to commit suicide in the relatively early stages of custody, mostly in the first three months, and approximately half of all prison suicides occur within the first six months of the sentence. Most inmate suicides, like West, come from a deprived family background typified by abuse and/or criminality, and have a history of violence and mental health problems. Being placed, like West, in isolation or dissociation units has also been shown to increase the risk of inmate suicide by altering the inmate's mental state. Prisoners in isolation are unable to communicate and discuss their suicidal feelings with others, which intensifies their anxieties.

Hanging is by far the most common form of suicide in prison, and is a fairly certain method of death, providing the victim can avoid discovery, and is certain that the rope and its support are strong enough. Disadvantages to the method include the fact that it can be very painful, depending on the kind of rope used, and the fact that there is a strong likelihood of brain damage if the victim is rescued before death. It has been estimated that Fred West would have died within five or six minutes of his hanging, but his body was not discovered until the guards returned at 1.00pm. Despite frantic attempts to revive him, West was declared dead at 1.22pm, thereby—much to the outrage of his victims' families—escaping a life behind bars.

West's suicide was obviously very carefully planned out, right down to his cheerful demeanour in the days leading up to it. It also bears many of the hallmarks of his other crimes —the obsessiveness, the collecting, the construction. Some have speculated that West deliberately chose hanging as a sexual method of suicide, since sadistic and masochistic rituals played an important part in his everyday life, as well as his crimes. The psychological motives behind his suicide are difficult to discern, since West appeared to have no sense of guilt over his crimes, and appeared to possess no moral or spiritual faculties. One motivating factor, however, seems to have been Rose's rejection of him not long after their arrest. Some claim she turned again him after realizing he was responsible for murdering their daughter Heather; others claim her rejection of him was a result of Fred implicating her far beyond her due.

What remains clear is that in the case of such an abnormal personality of Fred West, the motivation for his suicide remains as shadowy and obscure as the impulses behind bizarre and disturbing series of crimes.

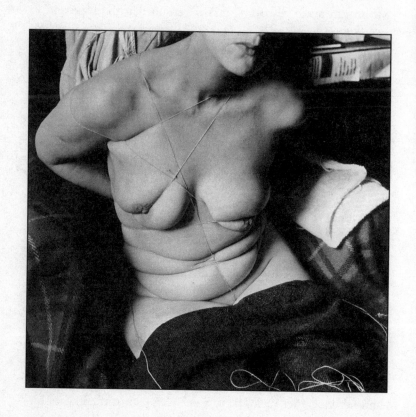

82

unica zurn

In 1953, Unica Zürn was living in Berlin. She was thirty-seven, a gifted short-story writer who had already achieved some success. She had great charm but was shy and secretive and suffered from attacks of schizophrenia. During the autumn she attended the opening of an exhibition organised by the dealer Rudolf Springer at the Maison de France on the Kurfurstendamm. The featured artist was Hans Bellmer, who had escaped from Nazi Germany to join the surrealists in Paris in 1938 and had subsequently made a strong but controversial reputation for himself with his photographs of an articulated doll and his meticulous drawings and engravings of young girls.[1] Bellmer was now fifty-one years old, and he immediately fell in love with this woman in a black suit with a large red rose in her buttonhole. Unica with her expressionless face, prominent nose and enormous eyes looked extraordinarily like Bellmer's doll, and Bellmer found the resemblance uncanny. The age-gap made no difference, for Unica was as fascinated with the author of the disturbing drawings in the exhibition as he was with her. Like Bellmer, she had been through an unhappy marriage, and had recently been divorced from her industrialist husband. And like Bellmer, she had lost two children in the divorce. The failure of her marriage had brought about her first schizophrenic attacks.

Unica lived with Bellmer in Berlin for some months. Bellmer was working on illustrations for *L'Anglais décrit dans les chateaux fermés* by André Pieyre de Mandiargues, and Unica was writing a book for Rudolf Springer, under Bellmer's encouragement, which consisted of ten anagrams with accompanying drawings. This was published in the summer of 1954 as *Hexentexte* (Witches' Writings) with a short post-face on anagrams by Bellmer.[2] Thirty copies contained a small original drawing by Bellmer. But life in Berlin was not easy. Bellmer was trying to support his ailing mother, and money was running out.

Soon after *Hexentexte* was published, Bellmer brought Unica to his home in rue Mouffetard, Paris, and introduced her to his friends. Living with Bellmer had its drawbacks, especially in such a tiny apartment and in such unattractive surroundings, but the two were to stay together until Unica's death sixteen years later. They made a strange couple: both always wore black, and Unica usually walked rather stiffly, a few paces behind Bellmer, his hair balding but with long hair at the back, so that one could picture them as Dr Coppelius and his doll Olympia in *The Tales of Hoffmann*. In their room they cooked on the tiny stove, filling the place with dreadful smells. Dust piled up because both refused to do any housework: she said she did not know about such things, and he was too lazy. They had very little money and in the early years they seemed to enjoy their misery together. The writer Constantin Jelenski found Unica extraordinary: "With her beautiful, pale, expressionless face and long black dress, she formed an essential part of Bellmer's life. It was an important relationship for both of them. Bellmer had been very lonely and appreciated her company enormously. In the tiny apartment, one felt how positive their relationship was, one of mutual admiration. Bellmer was very possessive, there was a strong sexual bond to begin with." [3]

Bellmer had great faith in Unica's abilities, and encouraged her to write and to draw. She had exhibitions of her paintings and drawings in Paris in 1956 and 1957 with catalogue notes and poems written by de Mandiargues, who remembered her as "charming and intelligent. Coming to Paris made her an artist: she was really the creation of Bellmer. They shared a pessimistic and romantic approach to their work. They had a sexual and spiritual relationship".[4] Unica's quirky, meticulous drawings of sexualised animal and human forms can be seen to relate to the images drawn by the insane, as well as having a lot in common with surrealist automatism, and they fascinated Max Ernst who wrote a text in a secret script inspired by them in the catalogue of her large Paris exhibition of 1962.[5] They also point to the instability of her health caused by her schizophrenia.

The relationship with Unica inspired strong images from Bellmer. He accentuated her expressionless, doll-like face in a careful pencil study inscribed *Für Unica, meine liebste Kieschen, Zum Andenken, Hans Bellmer, Berlin 1954*. A double portrait of 'Hans and Unica' of 1955 creates an astonishing image of Unica as a cephalopod, a woman consisting only of head and legs; she is meticulously painted in oils against a creamy background, and her face with its hollow cheeks and enormous eyes re-creates the doll, even down to the ribbon in the hair. This ribbon is collaged lace, as is most of her body. Pearls have been stitched on to the canvas along the edge of the lace, and one painted red is her nipple. The face of Bellmer himself with his cold, piercing eyes peers out of the collaged material as if contained inside the body of the cephalopod, as if totally fused with the beloved through the power of desire. The theme is taken further in a large drawing heightened with gouache paint dating from 1963: here, the Unica-cephalopod has Bellmer's dripping eye for an anus-vulva which recalls his illustrations for Georges Bataille's *Histoire de l'oeil*. The most astonishing images of Unica are a series of black and white photographs of 1958 which show her naked on a bed and in a chair, tied up with string which creates extraordinary folds and shapes in her flesh.[6] They were made with her full and enthusiastic co-operation. The inspiration came from a photograph of a murder victim which Bellmer had copied many years earlier. He now had the opportunity of experimenting with a real body and recording his experiments as he had previously recorded the metamorphoses of his doll. One image of murderous violence took on an abstract shape when Bellmer used it to illustrate the cover of *Le Surréalisme, Même*, issue four, Spring 1958, under the title 'Keep in a Cool Place'.

In December 1959 Bellmer's beloved mother died. She had stood by him throughout his life, and her loss was a terrible blow. From now on he became more and more dependent on Unica. He was lonely and needed her friendship and encouragement. Unica was also lonely, and she needed someone to believe in her talent. Her attacks of schizophrenia made life very difficult for him. She had no social graces and would make no effort to adapt herself to circumstances. She often treated Bellmer like a dog, but he would shrug his shoulders and put up with it, in a manner that recalls the masochism he exhibited so often. She appalled his friends by frequently insulting him in public; over the years, they became more and more isolated. He in turn was not easy to live with: his lifestyle was difficult for any companion to share, and he could be a real tyrant, forbidding Unica from playing her modern music on the gramophone and discouraging her contacts with male friends. Unica's attacks of schizophrenia were usually heralded by long accounts of her fantasies and childhood memories and by acts of senseless violence. When Bellmer needed peace and quiet to work, he would go to the studio flat of his old friend and confidante Herta Hausmann, where he found a much more congenial atmosphere.

The relationship between the two became bedevilled by their respective states of health: Unica was already showing signs of mental disturbance, and Bellmer was beginning to suffer from alcohol poisoning. Unica's first stay in hospital had been in 1957. In about 1960, she left Bellmer and returned to Berlin where her behaviour caused her to be committed to an asylum. Bellmer was desperately unhappy and finally managed to arrange her release and her return to Paris. In May 1962 she missed the opening of the exhibition of her drawings at the Point Cardinal Gallery because she was detained in the Sainte Anne Clinic where she suffered from the illusion that the poet and painter Henri Michaux was in love with her and was communicating with her telepathically. She spent many subsequent periods in this clinic, where Dr Lacan took particular interest in her case[7]; on certain occasions she was arrested when out on her own, and had to be collected from a police station, and once Bellmer had to have her taken away in a strait-jacket. In January 1963 Bellmer himself was in hospital for his first disintoxication cure, and his health was giving serious cause for concern. The year 1964 was one of real crisis for them both. They spent five months in a little house on the Ile de Ré near La Rochelle, their favourite holiday home, and for three weeks they were joined by Unica's daughter Katrin. Bellmer was suffering from alcohol poisoning and heart-trouble; Unica succumbed to a combination of sunstroke, intoxication ad over-excitement at recollections of her former life in Berlin, and had to be admitted to a psychiatric hospital in La Rochelle. Bellmer's desperation is clear from the almost daily letters he wrote to his friend Herta: "While Unica is with me, I have practically no friends. I am responsible for her, and I am sitting on a powder keg."; "Her mental activity has become completely unstable, she is getting thinner and thinner, she doesn't sleep easily and has dangerous fantasies"; "I don't see why I should ruin the years left to me. I've done all I can for five years. I can't do more"; "The sad Unica chapter is closed: very late in the day, for my personal health. How good to be able to concentrate on work."[8]

Bellmer however found it impossible to live without Unica and they therefore continued their relationship. They moved to a top-floor flat in the rue de la Plaine and he encouraged her in her writing. *Hexentexte* was published in a French translation as *Oracles et spectacles* in 1967 with a new illustration by Bellmer. Unica was working on *Der Mann in Jasmin* (The Man of Jasmine), an autobiographical study in the third person subtitled 'impressions of a mental patient, U.Z.' [9] This is a disturbing account of her periods in clinics and asylums and an examination of her own state of mind and her thoughts about 'the old enchanting land of death'. The Man of Jasmine was her childhood fantasy figure, a little girl's great hero, and when Unica first met Bellmer's friend Henri Michaux she believed him to be its incarnation. Her unreciprocated passion for Michaux precipitated the mental illness that dogged her last years: "A few days later she experiences the first miracle in her life: in a room in Paris she finds herself standing before the Man of Jasmine. The shock of this encounter is so great that she is unable to overcome it. From this day on she begins, very very slowly, to lose her reason."[10] She reveals a world of hallucinations in which acute states of depression alternate with powerful visions: "She is unaware that she is suffering from hallucinations. In her present state, the most incredible, hitherto unseen things become reality, so that when these images appear to her in the night sky, they are *really* there."[11]; "But she has already disappeared halfway into the abyss of a new, deep depression, as if that were the law of this illness. A few unusual days, a few nights filled with the shattering experiences of hallucinations, a short upward momentum, a feeling of being extraordinary – and afterwards the fall, reality, the realization that it had all been an illusion. She marches in the grey fifth column of the mortally depressed. The struggle of a medication against her state of delirium, this one short period which had made her madness worthwhile because it had rewarded her with new experiences – this struggle is quickly won by the medication."[12] The themes of death and suicide run through the narrative: "The small drop of courage, the short flicker of joy, has gone. As she steps on to the chair in order to place her neck in the noose, she sees two cats directing their large, beautiful eyes at her and studying her. And the cats yawn and stretch in all their dignity, beauty and distance, and above all their enormous indifference to the person standing there on the chair with her head in a noose. She feels ashamed of herself before these animals. She goes back to bed and begins to occupy herself with her body in a way which, several days later, proves to have disastrous consequences. As if the rumours she had heard as a child had turned true: If you do that you'll go blind, and end up paralysed!"[13] Her concern with finding appropriate language for her experiences leads her to experiment with anagrams as in her earlier *Hexentexte,* with astonishing results. The book was greeted with enthusiasm by critics and writers when it was published posthumously in 1971. Michel Leiris described it as the most important book he had read that year,[14] and Malcolm Green wrote later that it added "a further masterpiece to that small, precious row of unclassifiable works that includes Breton's *Nadja,* Nerval's *Aurélia,* Leonora Carrington's *Down Below* and Lautréamont's *Maldoror.*"[15]

For the moment, Unica needed someone to translate her text into French, and she turned to her friend Ruth Henry whom she had not seen for three years. Ruth later recalled how Unica had changed: "She sat hunched up in an armchair, a Gauloise always between her fingers, saying very little. She was so dosed with drugs that she moved as if in a catatonic trance. It was fortunate there was a lift in the building as she couldn't walk up stairs. Bellmer also found it difficult to walk. When we went out, I always had to help each of them out of the car with great care."[16]

With the encouragement of Ruth and Bellmer, Unica wrote another book, *Dunkler Frühling* (Dark Spring), in which she recounted her childhood memories of life in Berlin, once again in the third person.[17] She recalls games with two boys from her school who tie her to a post and fire at her with a bow and arrows: "The game is dangerous but it is what she wants. They blindfold her. They light a fire so close to her clothes that she begins to catch fire. They pull her hair, pinch her, punch her. No complaint escapes her lips. She suffers in silence, lost in masochist dreams where ideas of revenge and reprisals have no place. Suffering and pain give her pleasure. She pulls on her bonds and feels the ropes cut into her flesh with sensual delight."[18] She describes her father whom she adores but whom she rarely sees, her mother whom she hates and who makes sexual advances to her, and her elder brother who rapes her when she is ten. She discovers the pleasures of masturbation and she enjoys the sexual attentions of her dog. But her father is away and she wants to escape from her detested mother and brother: "She looks out of the window and thinks about her approaching death. She has decided to throw herself out of the window…She lies in her redskin tent which she has built in her bedroom, and looks at her treasures for the last time. Her father has given her a little Buddha, an Egyptian princess's bracelet and a Turkish cushion. She has a collection of glass marbles of all imaginable colours and a collection of silver paper rolled into six large balls….She climbs on to the windowsill, holds on to the shutter and looks once more at her shadow-like reflection in the mirror. She finds herself beautiful and slightly regrets her decision. 'It is finished,' she says in a quiet voice and she feels herself already dead before her feet leave the windowsill. She falls on her head and breaks her neck."[19] Malcolm Green has described the book as "a sombre masterpiece of forbidden childhood love and the painful awakening of sexuality".[20]

In September 1969 Bellmer had a severe stroke and was rushed to the Lariboisière hospital. The left side of his body remained paralysed for the rest of his life, and from now on he was a permanent invalid, spending most of his time in bed and only rarely going out in a wheelchair. Ruth remembered that life in the rue de la Plaine was now becoming unbearable. Bellmer and Unica lived on steak tartare, chocolate and vodka. Neither spoke a word to the other. Bellmer lay in bed all day in front of a television with the sound turned down. The French windows leading on to the little terrace on the top floor of the building had been smashed when Unica hurled an ashtray across the room. Each needed the support which neither could offer. Bellmer's physician, Dr Weiss, wanted peace and quiet for his patient; Unica's psychiatrist, Dr Rabain, warned that a crisis could come at any moment. Unica was taken to La Maison Blanche, a clinic at Neuilly-sur-Marne, just outside Paris. Ruth found her in a ward of sixty people: she was crying uncontrollably and begging to be taken away. She grabbed Ruth's jacket and lay on it to prevent her leaving. Her daughter Katrin arrived but refused Bellmer's request to take her back to Berlin, so Dr Rabain arranged for her to go to the private clinic at the Château de Chailles near Blois where Jacques Prévert's daughter had been well looked after a few years previously. Here the course of treatment brought about a rapid transformation, and she became lucid and even quite cheerful. But she was desperately worried about the future, for Bellmer had written her a final letter: "Our ways must definitely separate. Since your last nerve crisis in my flat, I have become more severely ill, and I am becoming more nervously depressed. The doctors have decided that we cannot live together. Your crises are too aggressive and powerful. And in my condition I am helpless. So I cannot and will not have you living with me anymore…We must get used to the fact that our relationship is now at an end. We cannot die together, we cannot live together. But we must remain dear to each other until we die. We can write to each other if circumstances make it possible. Will you do that, my dearest friend? Don't forget that I am thinking of your future. I embrace you. Farewell. Your dearest Hans." [21]

The situation for both Unica and Bellmer in that summer and autumn of 1970 was desperate. Each could not live without the other, yet they could no longer live together. Ruth and Herta visited both Unica and Bellmer as often as they could, but it was clearly not enough: Bellmer wrote to Herta in July: "For me, loneliness has become the hell of depression, fear and unhappiness. The separation from Unica, and the worries about her, take from me all taste for life, all hope. The result is my paralysis, my terrible debility. I am nearing the end. I would like

straight to hell

to die, but it would need to be in a sleep from which I would not wake. I am unable to work. Drawing would be the only means of relieving the pain of my thoughts."[22]

Unica was allowed to leave hospital for five days in October, in order to prepare for her new life outside, and Ruth invited her to stay. But when Sunday 18 October arrived, Ruth had influenza, and so Bellmer's friend and dealer André-François Petit collected Unica from the Château de Chailles. Unica asked Petit to drive her to Bellmer's flat rather than to Ruth, and he left her there in the afternoon. She had no suitcase or spare clothing, merely her handbag. "She was happy to see Bellmer again, relaxed, cheerful, too cheerful perhaps," said Petit later.[23] Bellmer and Unica spent a "pleasant evening of conversation in which they agreed that there could be no future for them together."[24] At ten o'clock next morning when the nurse was out shopping, "without any obvious sign of emotion, and clearly resolved to do what no-one could have guessed, nor prevented",[25] Unica picked up a chair, opened the French windows, crossed the terrace, climbed on to the chair, and jumped to her death. "It is finished, she says in a quiet voice and feels herself already dead before her feet leave the windowsill."[26]

Bellmer was too overwhelmed by grief to make funeral arrangements. Ruth took care of these. But he insisted, as an atheist, that there should be no cross on the coffin. He placed lighted candles all around the apartment, and sent a wreath of red roses (the flowers Unica had been wearing at their first meeting). He never recovered from her death. His already precarious state of health declined noticeably in the following months. He was taken to the private view of his retrospective exhibition at the Centre National d'Art Contemporain in November 1971, and his last journey was in the summer of 1974 to see a film-documentary on his work made by Catherine Binet. For the sequence featuring the doll photographs, she had made a soundtrack featuring a recording of Unica singing a German folk song interspersed with a twelve-year-old girl reading Paul Eluard's poems inspired by the doll. At this point in the film, Bellmer wept uncontrollably. He died on 24 February 1975. At his request he was buried beside Unica in the Père Lachaise Cemetery. The simple marble tomb is marked 'Bellmer-Zürn'. On top is a plaque inscribed with the words he wrote on her wreath: "My love will follow you into Eternity."

Was Unica the *creation* of Bellmer? Although he provided an inspirational environment, and introduced her to the fascination of anagrams, her writings are very clearly her own, and have met with much success in their posthumous German, French, English and Japanese editions. She benefited greatly from Bellmer's encouragement of her art, but her work was quite separate from his. Her gouaches and drawings reveal a very personal visionary world occupied by strange hybridised human and animal figures, executed in a meticulously detailed technique. While some have seen them merely as examples of the marginal art of the insane, others have related them to the automatism of surrealist dream-states, and she was included in the International Exhibition of Surrealism at the Daniel Cordier Gallery in Paris in 1959. Patrick Waldberg wrote of her art: "It is the cruel privilege of certain rare beings to know how to transmute anguish, nightmare and terror into absolute beauty."[27] Renée Riese Hubert, in her study of the Bellmer-Zürn relationship in *Magnifying Mirrors: Women, Surrealism and Partnership*, came to a memorable conclusion: "Though their works evince similar problematics, it would hardly be advisable to relate them in terms of mirrors and reflections. Their participation, however searching it may have been, is scarcely reducible to an idealized collaboration, for wounds and lacerations predominated in their artistic relatedness. Their art was indeed akin to flaying, with both of them playing the part of Marsyas skinned alive by Apollo."[28]

Was Unica the *victim* of Bellmer, as some commentators

have suggested?[29]The photographs which he took of her tied up with string were the product of a joint enterprise, and she had experienced pleasure from such masochistic activities long before knowing Bellmer, as detailed in *Dunkler Frühling*. Bellmer often refers to these aspects of Unica's personality in letters to his psychiatrist, Dr Ferdière: "There is a crucial problem in Unica's make-up: Masochism, which only very rarely is transformed (ascendant-schizophrenic crises) into its opposite."[30] In one letter, he reports Unica's remark: "It is not unhappiness which I fear; it is happiness which frightens me."[31] And yet he was well aware of the way some outsiders saw the relationship. In another letter to his psychiatrist, he wonders if he sensed a victim when he first met Unica, and concludes: "If Unica were to ask herself the same question, she would I think reply YES!"[32] Unica herself wrote in her Journal (in the third person): "Bellmer and her, comrades in misery since 1953, a great friendship… with a few shocks for her."[33] The attacks of schizophrenia had started in Berlin before she met him, and their source lay in her early family experiences and the break-up of her marriage.[34] During the last year of her life, she told Ruth in some detail about the superstitious fear instilled in her as a child of being horribly punished for masturbating which she recognised as lying at the root of her crises.[35] She also described how certain of her hallucinations were brought on by thoughts of Nazi atrocities and her guilt at being German.[36] She thought of killing herself on many occasions before meeting Bellmer, as her writings attest. Her suicide was clearly a planned and deliberate action, not done to punish Bellmer but to solve her problem, a ritual suicide in the home she had shared with the man she loved but could no longer live with.

[1] cf. Peter Webb with Robert Short, *Hans Bellmer,* Quartet Books, London, Melbourne and New York, 1985; Creation Books, London, 2004).
[2] Unica Zürn, *Hexentexte*, Galerie Springer, Berlin, 1954.

3 Interview between Constantin Jelenski and Peter Webb, Paris, 17 December 1983.

4 Interview between André Pieyre de Mandiargues and Peter Webb, Paris, 18 December 1983.

5 Catalogue of exhibition at Le Point Cardinal Gallery, Paris, 1962.

6 Reproduced in *Hans Bellmer, Photographe*, Centre Georges Pompidou, Paris, 1983, pp.117-127.

7 Cf. letter from Hans Bellmer to Constantin Jelenski, Paris, no date (c.1962-3).

8 Letters to Herta Hausmann, Il de Ré, 26 July, 29 July, 1 August, 5 August, 1964, author's
translation.

9 Unica Zürn, *L'Homme Jasmin, impressions d'une malade mentale*, translated by Ruth Henry and Robert Valançay, with preface by André Pieyre de Mandiargues, Gallimard, Paris, 1971; *Der Mann in Jasmin*, Ullstein, Frankfurt, 1977; *The Man of Jasmine*, translated by Malcolm Green, Atlas, London, 1994.

10 *The Man of Jasmine*, p.27.

11 Ibid, p.33.

12 Ibid, p.113.

13 Ibid, p.91.

14 cf. Ruth Henry, *Rencontre avec Unica*, in *Sombre Printemps*, Belfond, Paris, 1984, p. 108.

15 Malcolm Green, introduction to *The Man in Jasmine*, op. cit., p.18.

16 Interview between Ruth Henry and Peter Webb, Paris, 20 December 1983.

17 Unica Zürn, *Dunkler Frühling*, with three illustrations by Hans Bellmer, Merlin Verlag, Hamburg, 1969; *Sombre Printemps*, tr. Ruth Henry and Robert Valançay, frontispiece by Hans Bellmer, Belfond, Paris, 1971.

18 Ibid, p.23, author's translation.

19 Ibid, p.93;98-99, author's translation.

20 Malcolm Green, introduction to *The Man of Jasmine*, Atlas Press, London, 1994, p.11.

21 Letter from Hans Bellmer to Unica Zürn, Paris, 19 April 1970, author's translation.

straight to hell

[22] Letter from Hans Bellmer to Herta Hausman, Paris, 13 July 1970, author's translation.

[23] Cf. *Approche d'Unica Zürn*, Le Nouveau Commerce, Paris, 1981, no pagination.

[24] Interview between Herta Hausman and Peter Webb, Paris, 17 February 1984.

[25] Ruth Henry, *Rencontre avec Unica*, op.cit. p.120.

[26] See note 19.

[27] Patrick Waldberg, *La Femme Surréaliste*, Obliques, Paris, 1977, p.260.

[28] Renée Riese Hubert, *Magnifying Mirrors: Women, Surrealism and Partnership*, University of Nebrasaka Press, Lincoln and London, 1994, p.159.

[29] see for example Sabine Scholl, *Unica Zürn: Fehler Fallen Kunst*, Frankfurt am Main, 1990.

[30] Hans Bellmer and Unica Zürn, *Lettres au docteur Ferdière*, Seguier, Paris, 1994, letter of November 1964.

[31] Ibid, letter of 25 October 1964.

[32] Ibid, letter of 1 and 2 November 1964.

[33] *L'Homme Pourbelle* (Journal, also known as *Crécy*), in Unica Zürn, *Gesamtausgabe*, volume 5, Brinkmann und Bose, Berlin, 1989, p.179.

[34] see for example Dr Rabain in his essay in Unica Zürn, *L'Homme Jasmin*, op.cit., and Inge Morgenroth, introduction to Unica Zürn, *Das Weisse mit dem rotten Punkt*, Berlin, 1981.

[35] Cf. Ruth Henry, *Rencontre avec Unica Zürn*, op.cit. p.119.

[36] Malcolm Green, op cit, p.8.

diane linkletter

Everybody's heard the urban legend about some girl who, while under the influence of LSD, is killed when she jumps out of a window believing she can fly. This legend is often traced back to the case of the 20-year-old Diane Linkletter, who – according to popular belief – died after leaping from her apartment window after taking an enormous dose of LSD. The truth about Linkletter's death, however, is rather less spectacular than the legend – and certainly less bizarre than *The Diane Linkletter Story*, the short film that John Waters was inspired to make after her demise.

Diane Linkletter, who committed suicide in October 1969, was the youngest child of American television personality, author and columnist Art Linkletter. Even prior to his daughter's death, Linkletter was vitally concerned with what he saw as the eroding state of family values, and was actively engaged in lecturing across the country on the topic of "Permissiveness in This Society." Ironically, three months before Diane's death, the family had endured a similar loss when John Zweyer, husband of Linkletter's oldest daughter Dawn, had shot himself in the head in the back garden of his Hollywood home, having reportedly grown despondent over the failure of his insurance business.

According to her friend Katherine Oliver, Diana Linkletter had always been "searching for something she couldn't find." She had been depressed for many years, and eventually became desperately unhappy with her own life. During the early hours of 3 October 1969, she apparently became determined to end her sufferings. At 3am, sounding "very upset", she called a friend, Edward Durston, and begged him to come over to her West Hollywood apartment. When he arrived she baked some cookies, and the two friends sat up all night talking. Durston claimed Diane was in a "despondent, depressed, emotional state," that she was "concerned with her identity, her career," and because of her father's fame and reputation, "she could not be her own person."

At about 9am, according to Durston, Diane went into the kitchen and didn't return. When he went to look for her, Durston was horrified to see that Diane was climbing out of the kitchen window. He ran over and grabbed her by the belt of her dress, but the fabric ripped as Diane plummeted six floors to the street below.

So how did the story develop that Diana Linkletter leapt out of a window while under the influence of LSD?

Ironically, it was perpetuated by her father. Art Linkletter, who was giving a lecture on "The Permissive Society" in Colorado at the time of his daughter's death, claimed within hours of hearing about the tragedy that Diane had been under the influence of LSD when she jumped. "It isn't suicide, because she wasn't herself," he claimed. "It was murder. She was murdered by the people who manufacture and sell LSD." Linkletter made this statement – which was widely repeated in the press, and relied upon as the cause of Diane's death–before an autopsy had even been performed on his daughter's body.

For many years afterwards, Art Linkletter continued to describe his daughter's death as the result of a "bad LSD trip." He claimed that Diane had been experimenting with LSD for the last six months, and the night she died she was in the middle of an out-of-control drug experience. Later, after the results of Diane's autopsy were published, her father claimed that his daughter often experienced flashbacks from a bad trip taken six months earlier, and this must have panicked her into taking her own life. Yet those who knew Diane claim she'd never even taken LSD, and Edward Durston claims that on the night of her death she wasn't panicked, but simply overwhelmed, despondent and determined to end her suffering.

But why would Art Linkletter want to perpetuate the misapprehension that his daughter's suicide was LSD related? There are two answers to this question.

Firstly, Linkletter's campaign against the evils of the "permissive society" gained enormous attention from this sudden tragedy—his own, innocent daughter turned into a suicidal maniac after involving herself in the dark world of psychedelic drugs. Diane's death gave her father a new, important public role as a crusader in the war against psychedelics. He began to lecture ceaselessly on the topic, focusing his anger on Timothy Leary, the main advocate and guru of LSD. His daughter's death became symbolic of a tragedy that could be visited upon the home of any god-fearing American at any time—a tragedy caused by those evil fiends who manufacture and sell LSD to naïve young children.

Secondly, to claim that Diane was under the influence of a "bad trip" at the time of her death was to minimize her father's responsibility in the affair. Diane's depression was apparently a result, at least in part, of her inability to escape from her father's reputation, and her inability to lead a life of her own. To adopt a view of events that exaggerates the importance of outside factors upon the final outcome lessens Diane's own responsibility—and that of her family—for her actions. In this case, Art Linkletter clearly chose to deny or ignore evidence that his daughter committed suicide because she was terribly depressed, and instead to perpetuate the more comforting fiction that she killed herself because she was "out of her mind" on drugs. To acknowledge that his daughter's death was a suicide would also be to acknowledge that perhaps there was something he could have done to help prevent it.

Whether through denial or deliberate deception, Art Linkletter clearly chose to present his daughter Diane as a victim of society's evils, and not as an emotionally unstable young woman overwhelmed by the pressure to succeed, and by her own inability to make a mark on the world independent of her family. Perhaps his behavior makes more sense in the light of comments about Linkletter by those who've worked with him. In the words of one stagehand, "he is, without a single doubt, the most obnoxious, disgusting, miserable and hateful SOB I have ever encountered ... As the fight attendant in tears told me as I opened the door of the aircraft on which he arrived, ...'No wonder his daughter jumped out of the window.'"

Diane Linkletter obviously chose to leap from the window since it was clearly the most convenient suicide method to hand, especially since she was in the company of others who would have intervened to fetch help had she selected a more time-consuming technique, such as slitting her wrists or taking an overdose. However, jumping off buildings to commit suicide is a less popular method than the public imagination would believe, since it can be very frightening and requires great bravery.

For example, according to popular legend, during the Wall Street Crash of 1929 businessmen who had lost everything were throwing themselves out of their office windows into the street below. Most historians, however, will tell you that this never really happened. People only throw themselves *en masse* from a building when that building is collapsing or on fire. In the 1911 Triangle Shirtwaist factory fire in New Jersey, for example, more than fifty people jumped to their deaths from the ninth floor. The year before, nearly twenty people leaped from a burning tenement in Newark, New Jersey. In both cases, some people survived–or survived long enough–to explain why they had chosen to jump. Several said it was to make sure their bodies would be identified, and not incinerated beyond recognition. Perhaps this was the motive of many of those who leaped from the burning World Trade Center on September 11 2001, since they couldn't have known that the towers were about to collapse, destroying their bodies anyway.

The images of people leaping from the buildings are disturbing, but the experience itself may not actually have been so bad. People who've attempted suicide by jumping from the Golden Gate Bridge–and survived–report that the fall was experienced as almost transcendental, that it went in slow motion, that the experience was virtually mystical. Those who leaped from the World Trade Center on September 11 may have been jumping to certain death, but it would have been a death that annihilated consciousness in a way that was nearly instantaneous – far less painful, in fact, than the deaths most of us can look forward to.

The risk of fatality when leaping from a building is 90% for six stories, and increases the higher the drop. Diane Linkletter's kitchen window was six stories high, which is just about the minimum height to guarantee a certain death, though not necessarily a painless one. Nine out of ten people who fall six stories will die, but not always instantaneously. In most cases, however, even if death is not instantaneous, loss of consciousness will be, especially for those who land on concrete. Diane Linkletter died in hospital an hour and a half after her suicidal leap from injuries sustained in the fall; the official cause of her death was listed as "cerebral contusions, extensive; massive skull fracture, and multiple fractures of extremities". The toxicology report contained nothing unusual, showing that Diane had taken neither drugs nor alcohol the night of her suicide.

Diane Linkletter is buried in Forest Lawn Memorial Park, in Hollywood Hills. Her tombstone reads, "Darling, we loved you so much." Her father, now a columnist for coarse tabloid newspaper *The National Enquirer*, is perhaps best known for his catchphrase, "Kids do the darndest things".

yukio mishima

The infamous Japanese novelist, Yukio Mishima, celebrated worldwide and a future certainty for the Nobel Prize for Literature, had been contemplating and intricately planning his extravagant public suicide for at least three years before finally putting it into operation, in Tokyo on 25 November 1970. And in many ways, the origins of his sexually-inspired suicide had been launched twenty-five years earlier, with Imperial Japan's defeat and large-scale obliteration at the end of the Second World War, when endless hordes of American soldiers poured into the country's firestormed and A-bomb cities, humiliating and raping their populations before instituting the postwar regime of corporate excess and mass-prostitution which Mishima perceived as causing the irreparable desecration of the militaristic, divinely-inspired Japan that he had grown up within and loved. Even the glorious Emperor, Hirohito, who had commanded his loyal armies to invade and ravage the entire Asian landmass in the early 1930s and to set up human-experimentation and mass-extermination programmes such as Unit 731, had been humiliated and debased by the gum-chewing General Douglas MacArthur as he arrived to command the US Occupation of Japan. For Mishima, whose novels mixed imperial reverence with avant-garde sensibilities into an explosive sensory concoction, those profound humiliations and scars unleashed upon Japan coincided exactly with his realisation of his gay sexuality, and would re-emerge twenty-five years later – transformed and intensified – in his spectacularly mediatized suicide.

Mishima spent his final summer in the resort town of

straight to hell

Shimoda, to the south-west of Tokyo on the Izu peninsula – the very place in which the first American invasion of Japan had taken place in June 1853. He stayed in the luxurious Shimoda Tokyu Hotel with his family - although gay, Japanese social pressure had forced him to marry and produce two children - and spent his time sunbathing on the beach below the secluded hotel, finalizing the details of his suicide. On 1 August 1970, at Shimoda, Mishima finished his novel *The Decay of the Angel*, the last element in his multi-volume final work, *The Sea of Fertility*. Always a compulsive over-achiever, Mishima had intended to complete the book on the very morning of his suicide, but then finished it early in order to allow himself to make ever-more ambitious plans for his suicide, and to drop oblique hints to his friends of what he was about to do. Now forty-five years old, his muscular physique had started to fall apart, and the headlong bouts of buggery which had always propelled and fed into his creativity had now begun to exhaust him. His suicide was conceived as one that would lacerate the eye of the world and imprint the moment of his death on its retina forever. That outrageous death would be dedicated dually to the glorious nobility of the anus and to the now-castrated Imperial regime which had precipitated Japan into its near-obliteration of 1945.

In the final years of his life, Mishima had formed his own private, fascism-inspired army, the Shield Society, whom he regularly drilled on the slopes of Mount Fuji and on the roofs of the Tokyo department stores. Its sturdy young cadets, all in their late teens or early twenties and ripe for tenacious bouts of sake-fuelled militaristic sodomy, were chosen for their sheer obedience to Mishima and the dimensions of their sexual organs. He ensured that the Shield Society became celebrities, incessantly photographed by the Tokyo media in the suave, cock-hugging uniforms which Mishima had personally designed for his boys. Mishima chose four members of his private army – Hiroyasu Koga, Masakatsu Morita, Masahiro Ogawa and Masayoshi Koga

– to accompany him on his mission of death, although only one of the Shield Society cadets would actually die with him. Mishima and the four young acolytes spent the nights prior to Mishima's suicide in a top-floor suite of the Imperial Hotel, with a clear view of the vast parkland surrounding Emperor Hirohito's palace, engaged in a terminal, all-out session of patriotic sodomy which concluded only hours before Mishima's suicide.

On the morning of 25 November 1970, Mishima returned to his colonial-style house in southern Tokyo and left the manuscript of *The Sea of Fertility* for his publisher to collect; he exchanged pleasantries with his family and neglected to mention to his wife and children that he was about to eviscerate himself before having his head bloodily hacked from his body. The four Shield Society cadets picked him up in a car and, dressed in their uniforms, they sang gangster songs together as they headed for the military headquarters of Ichigaya, in central Tokyo, where Mishima was able to secure a private meeting with the commander. The Shield Society cadets promptly took the commander hostage and instructed him to order all of the staff and soldiers to assemble in the courtyard in front of the building. Mishima then stepped onto the balcony outside the commander's office and lengthily harangued the disinterested soldiers about how they had to return to the Imperial Way and reject the corporate stupor that would come to saturate Japan in the next decades (the speech was recorded and the film-maker Shuji Terayama used it as the soundtrack for one of his films). The soldiers hooted with derision, and, just after noon, Mishima returned to the commander's office in a state of fury. He stripped off his uniform, knelt down naked and sliced open his stomach horizontally with a knife designed explicitly for the purpose; his intestines slid from the deep rip, ran over his penis and gathered into a reeking pool of black blood and meat on the silk carpet. Mishima then urgently gestured for Masakatsu Morita to decapitate him, but the nervous cadet botched the operation, inflicting a wild series of clumsy hacking strokes around the bones of Mishima's neck and shoulders which caused him to wail in agony. Torrents of blood flew out in every direction, caking the walls. Finally, the more-blasé cadet Hiroyasu Koga pushed Morita aside and swiped off the head of the now-convulsed and sobbing Mishima with one expert sword-blow; Morita knelt down and Koga unhesitatingly handed out the same treatment to him. The room looked like a slaughterhouse.

As soon as Mishima and Morita were dead, the surviving cadets immediately freed the commander and allowed the excited Tokyo media to stream into the room; the press photographers scooped up Mishima's head from where it had rolled into a corner of the room and carried it by the ears, back to the silk carpet where the remainder of the still-gurgling body continued to expel floods of arterial blood. They placed the now-blackening head upright on the carpet and took flash photographs; the expression of utter horror on Mishima's face at the botched glory of his suicide was clearly evident. For the next twenty-five years, Mishima's widow Yuko attempted to distract attention from the determining element of noble sodomy in her husband's suicide, suggesting instead that Mishima had died in a state of temporary derangement; but with her own death on 31 July 1995 (and that of Mishima's brother, Chiyuki, in the following year), a tidal wave of manuscripts and letters began to emerge in which that determined and intricately-prepared suicide finally appeared in its authentic light: as a terminal crash of sodomy, fascism and obsessive creation, designed to disconcert and provoke the citizens of Japan for centuries to come.

david koresh

While locals in the Waco area found the Branch Davidians a harmless and friendly group, David Koresh had long attracted the suspicions of the FBI; they found his cult dubious and questionable, especially in its independence from the wider social structure. The Branch Davidians did not pay taxes, kept their children out of school, and, at least according to local rumor, owned a significant stockpile of weapons. Although agents who had been observing Koresh had plenty of opportunity to arrest him alone, on one of his frequent outings into town, they decided to make a raid on the complex, and see what kinds of weapons the cult possessed. This proved a disastrous move, leading to the deaths of four federal agents and six members of the sect, all killed in a violent gun battle.

After this initial raid, the FBI blockade began in earnest, leading to a 51-day standoff between the Branch Davidians and agents of the U.S. Bureau of Alcohol, Tobacco and Firearms who were trying to execute arrest and search warrants against Koresh because of reports that his group was stockpiling illegal weapons. Government vehicles surrounded the compound, demanding that the Davidians vacate their headquarters and offer themselves up for arrest. Koresh and his sect, however, were trapped in a religious dilemma. They believed that they needed to remain together until Koresh had completed his interpretation of the Seven Seals in the Biblical book of Revelation. In the end, the cult decided they should stand by their religious faith no matter what it cost. They believed there would be a peaceful end to the confrontation, convinced that Koresh would be able to finish his

straight to hell

interpretation while the FBI waited quietly outside the compound. There was no talk of suicide until the cultists felt they were about to be attacked.

At this point, Koresh began to discuss the possibility of suicide, and his comments were recorded on tape. During the 51-day siege of the cult compound, U.S. agents had managed to install listening devices inside the sect's complex by hiding them in containers that delivered milk to the children. These devices picked up snatches of conversations inside the compound from March 6 until about 11.45 am on April 19, during the final minutes of the siege.

The tapes made by surveillance microphones reveal that nobody in the compound was being held against their will, and that there was no evidence of physical or sexual abuse of children, although there are suggestions that the Branch Davidians were in possession of a number of automatic weapons. The tapes also reveal that the Davidians were deeply grounded in their religious beliefs, and convinced that Koresh was a divinely appointed leader who held the key to the book of Revelations – also known as the book of the Apocalypse.

Two days before the catastrophic inferno, FBI tanks began removing parked vehicles from around the Branch Davidian complex. To the Davidians, this was an important signal. Koresh had recently begun to experience prophecies of a violent end to the siege, and when FBI tanks began to move in threateningly, the cult interpreted this as a sign that these prophecies were about to come true. The FBI tapes include a conversation recorded at this time between Koresh and his first lieutenant, Schneider.

"They could bring the fire trucks," claims Schneider, "but they couldn't even get near us."

"That's all right," replies Koresh, and makes a sound imitating gunfire.

The following day – the day before the inferno – the

Branch Davidians begin discussing the possibility of whether they would be killed by fire, or whether god would allow them to survive.

"We'll run through the fire," claims one man on the tape.

"God wants us to do this?" asks a woman.

"That's what David said to do," replies Schneider, "and it's fine with me. Wherever you want to be … all his ways are directed, as far as I'm concerned."

"That's no fun," replies the woman.

"Oh no," says Schneider. "Nothing ever is."

That same day, Koresh told an FBI negotiator, "Your commanders are fixing to ruin the safety of me and my children."

"I think that was something that you brought," responds the negotiator.

In the same conversation, Koresh claims that forthcoming events would "place this in the history books as one of the saddest days in the world."

On the following day, April 19 1993, the apocalypse began, just as Koresh had prophesied. An FBI tank ploughed deep into the compound to inset tear gas into a room in which women and children had taken refuge. A number of fires broke out simultaneously, some of them possibly started by the Davidians, who are believed to have been in possession of various pyrotechnic devices. Survivors of the siege, however, claim that if the Davidians were indeed responsible for any of these fires, it was an act of deliverance, rather than suicide. Apparently, they believed that the flames would function as a wall of fire with which god would protect them from the assault while Koresh completed his interpretation of the Seven Seals. Instead, about eighty of the Branch Davidians were killed in the siege, most of them from the effects of the fire, but some, including five children, as a result of gunshots.

"My work is finished," claimed cult leader David Koresh, a month before his suicide. "I don't need to hang around here.

straight to hell

I've already been shot, understand? I've been rejected … All I need to do is cover it, cock the pistol back, have my thumb on the trigger and my mouth on the Psalms." One month later, as promised, instead of burning alive in the flames like his devoted followers, Koresh committed suicide by shooting himself in the head as fire consumed the Branch Davidian compound. An autopsy revealed he had died from a bullet wound to the brain. Next to him was his chief lieutenant, Steve Schneider, who had also shot himself in the head. Although both Koresh and his trusty lieutenant had opted for the traditional suicide method of a bullet in the brain, their deaths, according to Davidian creed, were not acts of self-murder, but of redemption.

donald cammell

"The only performance that makes it, that really makes it, that
makes it all the \tab way, is the one that achieves madness"
–Turner (Mick Jagger), in *Performance*

Hollywood, shabby Shangri-La of the doomed and disillusioned,
has always been a natural breeding ground for extravagant
gestures of self-destruction. Failed British starlet Peg Entwistle,
who famously leaped from the Hollywood sign, is only the most
symbolic icon of Tinseltown suicide. Countless fragile egos and
delicate nervous systems, unable to cope with the vicissitudes of
Los Angeles's cruelest industry followed Peg into willed
extinction.

Few of these exits can rival the bizarre death scene played
out in the bedroom of the gifted but ill-starred British film director
Donald Cammell in 1996. Cammell's sparse but visionary body
of work – only four feature films completed in a jinxed twenty-
eight year career – was never honored with any awards. But if the
Academy of Motion Picture Arts and Sciences ever hands out an
Oscar for Best Suicide, Cammell will surely be one of the
nominees. The *pièce de résistance* of a virtuoso whose films linger on
images of guns, transfigurative death, and the thin line between
love and lunacy, Cammell's self-murder was a restatement of all
of the themes that nourished his uncompromising imagination. A
Wildean aesthete who consciously crafted a fascinating *objet d'art*
out of the raw material of his existence, Cammell appears to have
designed his demise as the final flourish in a life dedicated to the
obsessive study of the act of violence as ritualistic work of art.

straight to hell

At 9:45 in the evening of April 24, 1996, China Kong, wife of the 62-year old filmmaker, was writing in the couple's office in their modest home atop the Hollywood Hills. Cammell entered the room, silently set some papers on China's desk, and headed for their bedroom. These documents included a letter addressed to China which freed her from any blame for the act he was about to perform. The next thing she heard was a gunshot. Cammell fired his ever-present 9mm Glock pistol at his forehead, but was still alive and fully conscious. After calling 911, China knelt beside her husband to comfort him while they waited for the ambulance to arrive.

Despite the entrance wound gushing blood from his forehead, she found Cammell in the best of spirits, speaking to his wife with a serenity that bordered on happiness. The trauma may have brought on a tranquilizing shock, although some have speculated that he was simply elated at reaching the brink of the oblivion for which the manic-depressive director so frequently longed.

He calmly reminisced to his wife about the final scenes of his first and most famous film *Performance* (1968), an identity-blurring mystical tale of the violent collision between Chas (James Fox), a macho gangster on the lam and Turner (Mick Jagger), a burnt-out rock star who offers the criminal an uneasy sanctuary in his decadent London household. When Chas's hiding place is discovered by vengeful partners in crime who arrive to escort him to his execution, Turner asks to come with him on his journey. In an exchange of dialogue rich with double meanings, Chas replies "You don't know where I'm going." "Yes I do," says Turner. Fulfilling an implicit death pact that has been simmering since their first encounter, Chas fires his pistol at Turner's head. In one of the film's many bravura shots, Cammell shows us the bullet's perspective as it whirls through Turner's brain. We have the sense that this is not simple murder, but the fulfillment of Turner's yearning for liberating death. A glimpse of Turner's corpse crumpled in a closet reveals blood trickling from the head wound, in the same spot as Cammell's own fatal injury.

Gun nut Cammell certainly knew enough about the mechanics of firearms to realize that the most certain guarantee of instant death would be a shot to the brain fired upwards through the mouth. Was the mode of Cammell's suicide a recreation of his character Turner's fate? Chris Rodley, director of a documentary about Cammell's life, told journalist Mick Brown, "It's all there in *Performance*. I don't think it's far-fetched to suggest that *Performance* was a kind of rehearsal. Because [Cammell] read up so much on guns...he knew exactly what he was doing. I think that was absolutely intentional. I think it was stage-managed; the last performance."

This theory is supported by one of the cryptic comments Cammell made to his wife as he lay dying: "Do you see the picture of Borges?" In the scene that portrays Chas's murder of Turner in *Performance*, Cammell inserted a quick flash of the face of Argentinean author Jorge Luis Borges, whose enigmatic short stories exploring the interface between illusion and reality greatly influenced the filmmaker's own vision.

Cammell brought his favorite pistol to his many futile meetings with producers, a concealed threat that expressed his contempt for Hollywood's "misbred grey executives". Considering the ordeals he'd suffered at the hands of movie money men, it's surprising that the director didn't turn his gun on one of them instead of himself. Cammell's tendency to play recklessly with his revolver was a source of alarm to his friends; his habit of sleeping with the beloved weapon under his pillow was especially disconcerting.

Cammell made two final requests as he waited to die; he asked China for a pillow, so that the carpet wouldn't be "fucked up" by the blood pouring from his head. Then he asked her to hold a mirror before his face, so that he could scrutinize his death with the same calm concentration with which he voyeuristically observed the equally disturbing scenes he'd arranged before his camera. Cammell often mentioned to friends that he was born under Edinburgh's Victorian camera obscura lens located in Outlook Tower, through which sightseers regard the refracted reflection of the Scottish capital. He saw this as an omen of a career in the visual arts, first as a portrait painter and then as a filmmaker. On a more macabre note, Cammell's mirrored death echoes another scene from one of his films, 1988's *White Of The Eye*, in which a serial killer forces one of his victims to watch her death in a looking glass. Cammell said of the film that "the killer has a painter's eye, which I suppose is mine." It was a fitting end for an artist intrigued with the disorienting metaphysics of reflection, in cinema and in life.

Cammell's last film, *Wild Side*, co-written with China, includes a harrowing scene of a suicide attempt carried out in the presence of a key character's lover. In the film, the would-be suicide is a sexually adventurous Chinese woman (Joan Chen), and the desperate witness is her gun-toting, unstable boyfriend (an Elvis-like Christopher Walken). In one of those role reversals so beloved of Cammell, the dire scene played in his bedroom found a sexually adventurous Chinese woman (his wife, China) witnessing the death of her gun-toting, unstable husband (Cammell).

Cammell's protracted dying lasted forty-five minutes after the trigger was pulled. In a stroke of absurdity well-suited to his own black humor, his life would probably have been saved had not the ambulance driver lost his way while searching for Cammell's house obscurely nestled in the winding roads of the Hollywood Hills.

News of Cammell's suicide was hardly reported; apart from his brief notoriety after the release of *Performance*, he was known only to a small cult following. In the intervening years, however, that cult has expanded – his untimely death has granted strange new life to his small but increasingly influential legacy.

According to his wife, "Donald always said his work would be appreciated far more after his death."

Although those who only knew Cammell superficially were shocked by the suicide of the outwardly charming, humorous and engaging raconteur, his closet companions appear to have viewed his passage as an inescapable fate. Apparently Cammell kept his inner torment well concealed from strangers. "I knew things were going to happen the way they happened for a very long time, some 20 years," said China, who'd been his closest collaborator and muse since an illicit passion developed between the forty-year old director and herself when she was only fourteen. In 1998, Cammell's friend and fellow filmmaker Kenneth Anger, never shy in proclaiming his prophetic powers, declared, "I predicted Donald Cammell's suicide. He was in love with death." Cammell's morbid nature inspired Anger to cast him as the Egyptian death god Osiris in his own *Lucifer Rising*.

David Cammell, the director's brother, claimed that his sibling entertained fantasies of suicide from the age of seven. Cammell's long-time lover, model Myriam Gibril, who served as the director's muse before his romance with China, split from Cammell due to the psychic pressure exerted by his constant threats of suicide.

Whatever neurological disability may have beset Cammell, there can be no doubt that the environmental factors of his extraordinarily luckless career must have exacerbated the condition. His only bona fide masterpiece, *Performance*, filmed in 1968, was shelved by Warner Brothers until 1971. Expecting Swinging London froth for the teen market, Warners balked at the disturbing picture, which was condemned by one studio rep as "something evil." The production process was besieged by the meddling of philistine movie biz administrators, horrified by *Performance*'s portrayal of casual violence, drugs, and sexual ambiguity. Upon the film's release, in a heavily cut form, most reviewers savaged *Performance*, and its critical reputation as one of the era's most important films wasn't established until years after its release. Typical was *The New York Times*'s denunciation of Cammell: "[His] name does not deserve to live on even in ignominy". Adding insult to injury, when the film gradually developed cult success, credit was invariably given to the film's co-director, Nicolas Roeg, whose career blossomed in stark contrast to Cammell's own declining fortunes. (Cammell's since been acknowledged as the principal creative force driving *Performance*, whereas Roeg is viewed as primarily responsible for the film's technical and cinematographic finesse.)

After moving to Los Angeles – an environment eminently unfit to the refined director's sophistication – he was forced into accepting the thankless identity of a journeyman director, taking what work he could find. He earned his living writing unproduced screenplays and was even reduced to filming rock videos – a form he practically invented in *Performance*. His frequent involvement with the notoriously fickle Marlon Brando led him to dissipate his energy on a series of never produced vehicles designed for the temperamental actor. The mediocre science fiction of 1977's *Demon Seed* was ill-suited to his gifts, and only *White Of The Eye* and *Wild Side* reveal something of the early promise of *Performance*.

In many ways, the disastrous circumstances surrounding his 1994 swan song *Wild Side* led directly to his undoing. An updated reworking of some of the criminal and erotic themes investigated in *Performance*, *Wild Side* showcased Cammell's best work in decades. However, the production company responsible for the film drastically truncated the final cut, reducing Cammell's vision to a shoddy exploitation programmer dumped without fanfare onto the video and cable market.

Cammell insisted on removing his name from the film, consequently spiraling into a deep depression. Despite the sexually omnivorous Cammell's own penchant for extramarital dalliances with young women, his misery was worsened by

China's affair with a younger man met on the set of *Wild Side*, which led her to leave their home. Even prior to this, Cammell's increasingly florid idiosyncrasies alienated China – his personality fractured, a secondary persona he dubbed the "uncensored Don" was granted full rein. Uncensored Don was given to such manic behavior as hopping in his car totally naked and speeding down a freeway. It's a testament to the director's often described charisma that he managed to charm himself out of this situation without being arrested when the police pulled him over.

Abandoned by his wife, his comeback film mangled into an embarrassing mess, and sliding into poverty as he was viewed as unbankably erratic, Cammell's always unstable mood sunk deeper into despair. He was persuaded by his brother to see a psychiatrist but quickly cut off his anti-depressant medication, complaining that it only worsened his frame of mind. But unpredictably, a false dawn began to illuminate Cammell's long night of the soul, seemingly pulling him back from the abyss.

In early 1996, China returned to Cammell's home, and they began collaborating on the screenplay for an underworld thriller concerning the Turkish-French heroin syndicate of the early 1930s. The script was hailed as his most accomplished and most potentially commercial work in years. April 22, 1996, he learned from his agent that the film could soon be moving into pre-production. Perversely, it was immediately on the heels of this welcome news that Cammell shot himself.

One grotesquely ironic development in the wake of Cammell's death was the 1997 re-release of a much-ballyhooed "director's cut" version of his aborted film *Wild Side*. Ari Lerner, the craven producer who had previously refused to issue Cammell's cut in 1994 – precipitating the director's final depression – now proudly unveiled a restored version under the title *Donald Cammell's Wild Side*. This attempt to cash in on the publicity that accrued after the director's suicide was cynically repackaged by the ghoulish Lerner as a "tribute" to the late Cammell. Previously unknown actress Anne Heche, featured as a bisexual call girl in the film, had recently made headlines, outing herself as lesbian comedian Ellen Degeneres' lover, thus upping *Wild Side*'s previously negligible marketability. The film, restructured from its previously butchered state, went on to be acclaimed as a minor classic, a posthumous testament to a tragically wasted genius who never recoiled from the performance that achieves madness.

hart crane

If suicide is in part the attempt to create an imaginary rather than biological death, and one in which control is retained over the method of dying, then the imaginative autonomy involved in both processes may help explain why the creative sensibility is so attracted to suicide. Imagination, which Hart Crane possessed to an extraordinary degree, not only dissolves the boundaries between inner and outer realities, but also invests the poet with the power to recreate the world on his own terms. Living antisocially, the poet may choose to die in a similar way, his death shaped by inner design and not the dictates of nature or the intervention of medicine.

Hart Crane lived and wrote like liquid explosive. The only child of a broken marriage – his father was a candy manufacturer in Ohio – Hart's conflictual and traumatic early years were spent siding with a highly-strung, hysterical mother in a distraught marital arena. Encountering his first gay experiences in his teens, ironically it is suggested with a friend of his father's, he renounced formal education to pursue poetry and his ideal of the perfect sailor with all the reckless abandon of someone on fast-burn.

It could be argued that the incandescent momentum of Crane's life wouldn't anyhow have allowed for a long life. Crane with his Rimbaudian belief in self-induced altered states, ran at life with the same dedication to overkill that had him at the age of 32 pitch over the stern of the Orizaba into the Caribbean. The reputation for bingeing that earned him the sobriquet "the roaring boy", in imitation of Christopher Marlowe's drunken brawls in

straight to hell

London pubs, pursued Crane from New York to Paris to Mexico, via innumerable prison cells.

Crane's dynamic was a visionary one that smacked poetry into another dimension. Hyping himself up by listening to Ravel's *Bolero*, played on endless repeat, his system catching fire from bottleneck slugs of Cutty Sark, Crane's early poems collected in *White Buildings* were the product of big city excitement launch-padded from an inherently romantic sensibility. The work is charged by the ability to compress sensory experience into its exact metaphorical equivalent. If Crane's book-length poem *The Bridge*, begun in the mid-1920s, sometimes finds comparison with T. S. Eliot's *The Waste Land*, both writers transforming the long poem into a collage of cultural references, then Crane's investment in the epic is invariably neural, whereas Eliot's is almost unfailingly cerebral.

Crane, like his prototypical model in visionary poetics, Arthur Rimbaud, was a distinctly neural poet, by which I mean he wired the poem with his own highly idiosyncratic nervous signature. All of his generosity as a person, his omnivorous sexual appetite, his widescreen expectations of life, together with a sensitivity continuously shattered by poverty and personal crises, come together in a poetry that polarises sensation as the nuclear core of its energy. Crane sometimes give the impression of entering a poem like someone throwing a window open above Bleeker St and being thrown back inside by the sonic roar of edgy traffic. The slightly tilted axis to many of his poems gives them a sense of having been written while the poet was nursing the residue of a hangover.

Crane organised his largely chaotic personal life around his poetry. Working variously as an advertising copy writer, a private secretary to a wealthy Californian businessman, and travelling whenever the opportunity permitted, the pattern of his fragmented, discontinuous existence finds its interface in the equally upended structure of his epic, in which dazzling lyricism compensates for lack of a realised theme. Crane's particular mind-set was best suited to working in short periods of hypercreativity, rather than through the sustained momentum he attempted to achieve in writing a long poem to give voice to his vision of the American Dream.

Crane's life was burnt by worry. Not only was there constant financial anxiety from his irregular earnings, but there were the exacting traumas surrounding his mother's second divorce in 1926, with which to contend. Her parasitical emotional dependency demanded of him that he wrote to her every day. He also had the problem of his sexuality and how best to accommodate it to the society in which he lived. In 1924 he had fallen in love with a young, blond Danish naval officer, Emil Opffer, who was to be the inspiration for 'Voyages', Crane's extraordinarily beautiful sequence of poems published in *White Buildings*, in which his love of maritime imagery is fused to an elegiac homoerotics of desire. Expanding on the nature of the relationship in a letter written to Jean Toomer, Crane wrote, 'I have never been given the opportunity for as much joy and agony before. The extreme edges of these emotions were sharpened on me in swift alternation until I am almost a shadow. But there is a conviction of love – that is the only way I can name it – which has somehow arrived in time, and which has (now so much has proved it) an equal basis in the both of us.'

It's the catch of honesty in Hart's account that jolts one into an awareness of his highly evolved individuality, as well as the sense of him seeking the same qualities in love as he does in art. Writing to his friend Waldo Frank about the visionary experiences imparted by his love for this handsome sailor, Crane wrote, 'It will take many letters to let you know what I mean when I say that I have seen the Word made Flesh. I mean nothing less, and I know now that there is such a thing as indestructibility. In the deepest sense, where the flesh became transformed through intensity of response to counter-response, where sex was beaten out, where a purity of joy was reached that included tears.'

Crane's letters are so directly complementary to his poetry, that they provide a continuous biographical commentary on the circumstances under which individual poems were written. The entire force of the man is present in both, his elated and agonised moods contending in a volatile cocktail of sensory experience. The arc of his poetry, payloaded with visionary allusions, is like his response to love, no matter how short-lived or brutal. The request is ultimately, as in 'Voyages 11', to 'Bequeath us to no earthly shore until/ Is answered in the vortex of our grave/ The seal's wide spindrift gaze toward paradise.'

The intimation of suicide here in the reference to being swallowed by a marine vortex, was to prove self-prophetic, as though Crane even at the time of celebrating his love for Emil Opffer was clear as to what form his end would take. There's every reason to believe that by living with the inner configuration of his death, Crane moved inevitably towards its physical resolution. If you decide you're going to take your own life, you're usually aware not only of how you will do it, but of having in the process activated an impulse that may or may not gather momentum. Crane's did, and his suicide may have been as much motivated by the need to be free of the presentiment, as it was an act of liberation from a set of acute emotional problems.

What Crane took with himself into the ocean was that rare thing, the selfless vision of the artist prepared to sacrifice himself unconditionally for his vision, a conviction nowhere better pronounced than in a letter written to his father about his artistic intentions. With characteristic generosity, Crane wrote, 'try to imagine working for the pure love of simply making something beautiful, - something that maybe can't be sold or used to help sell anything else, but that is simply a communication between man and man, a bond of understanding and human enlightenment –which is what real work is...I only ask to leave behind me something that the future may find valuable, and it takes a bit of sacrifice sometimes in order to give the thing that you know is yourself and worth giving. I shall make every sacrifice toward that end.'

Crane's 32 years carried with them all the impacted power and compression of someone attempting not only to make sense of himself in relation to his age, but also of the absolute themes favoured by the Elizabethans, life, love and death. Any life, no matter how long or productive, offers no more than a quick, close-up bite of the apple, and Crane took his lick fast and clean.

Gifted with a Guggenheim fellowship of two thousand dollars in March 1931, ostensibly to write a long poem on Cortez, Crane headed to Mexico on the Orizaba, the same ship from which he would jump into the Caribbean on his return journey a year later in 1932. Once in Mexico, and dressed unequivocally to cruise in a red sweater, white sailor pants and a blue silk handkerchief, his recklessness increased in proportion to his drinking. According to his friend and neighbour Katherine Anne Porter, Hart was desperate to live out the full spectrum of his sexual fantasies. 'He confessed that his sexual feelings were now largely a matter of imagination, which drove and harried him continually, creating images of erotic frenzy and satisfactions for which he could find no counterpart in reality…He said, he now found himself imagining that if he could see blood, or cause it to be shed, he might be satisfied.'

Beginning to burn up on heavy drinking and literally risking his life in picking up men on the streets, Hart suffering from acute loneliness, and having drunk away the first instalment of his grant, turned both paranoid and suicidal. Faced by a paralysing creative impotence, and still lacking any clear focus on his intended Mexican epic Crane found himself pinned by his old self-destructive habits. To the poet Leon Felipe Camino, who discovered him drunk and emoting to records by Marlene Dietrich, 'he was tall and had an angelic face, with large blue eyes filled with asombro: fright, astonishment, amazement.'

Crane's terror was of course of himself and the often
unmanageable contents of his imagination, as much attuned to
the dark as it was the light. It wasn't easy to be Hart. His
sensitivity had him live outside his skin most of the time, and
nobody can stay there longer than is tolerable. Death 'with a
bang' was what he had predicted for himself, and in Mexico he
worked himself towards the explosion.

Taking up with Malcolm Cowley's estranged wife, Peggy,
who had also joined Mexico City's expatriate colony as a
Guggenheim fellow, Crane driven by extreme loneliness attached
himself to Peggy first as a companion, and later as a confused,
distraught lover. Their mutually alcoholic and incongruous
relationship was to increase Hart's sense of guilt at betraying his
mother's affection by contact with another woman. Both wanting
to reform himself, and at the same time deeply resentful of any
changes made to his sexual orientation, Crane oscillated between
the desire to prove himself to Peggy and the need to cruise for
sailors after dark. 'She thinks she can reform me, does she? I'll
show her. Why, God damn her, I'd rather sleep with a man any
time than with her!' he railed in a letter, while informing his old
friend William Underwood that 'The fluttering gait and the
powder puff are unheard of here, but that doesn't matter in the
least. Ambidexterity is all in the fullest masculine tradition.' But
the climate wasn't quite as accommodating as Crane made it
sound, and on 28 January 1932, her spent a drunken night in jail
for having sex with a servant boy in public, and with Peggy
refusing to visit him, he was released the following day with a
severe warning, and a ban on him ever entering Taxco again.

Peggy Cowley's memories of her short-lived liaison with
Crane are additionally interesting for the light she throws on his
feverish moods of creativity. Hart's year in Mexico triggered little
more than one completed poem, 'The Broken Tower,' but Peggy
was witness to its creation, and the combustible assault Crane

made on his material. Elated by the pre- Christmas festivities, in which tribal rituals had been performed in the early hours before the cathedral, and by the pyrotechnical firework displays on Christmas day, to celebrate which he had bought 200 scarlet and green poinsettias, Crane was inspired to work on what was to be his last poem. Rather like Jackson Pollock's dynamic of running at the canvas, or Francis Bacon's habit of throwing paint at it to initiate a beginning, Crane furiously scribbled fragments on sheets of paper that were torn up and discarded. Writing to the sound of music played at full volume, and fired by the rush of tequila as it came up, Crane worked at the sort of manic pitch that burnt. Endlessly trying and changing phrases out loud, he was in Peggy" words, "he instrument on which he played the words, changing each perhaps a hundred times before retaining a small fragment.'

For three days Hart's energies raged as the poem began to be licked into tentative shape. With Peggy integral to its direction, Crane was interrupted in his work by having to return to Mixcoac to address practicalities connected with the disappearance of his passport, and by the need to be vaccinated against typhoid. Unable to sublet his house, and in urgent need of immediate money from his father's trust, he returned to Peggy and Taxco, with the poem still big in his head. It was there like a fireball, when unable to sleep, he went out on a night walk to the town plaza and stumbled across his friend the old Indian bell-ringer who was on his way to the church to announce the dawn. Requesting Hart assist him in his epiphanic work, the two men climbed the turrets of Santa Prisca and released the bells, or in Hart's poem, 'Oval encyclicals in canyons heaping/ The impasse high with choir.' The triumphant physical act of bell-ringing became for Crane the symbol of his return to a visionary dynamic, his reawakening to the call of poetry. The tower, a metaphor in Crane's mind for the one in which Danae in hiding had been impregnated by Zeus' golden shower, was now the receptacle of a poem brought powerfully alive by his memory of light breaking over the mountains as he had manipulated the bell ropes. With the act forming a gateway to the rebirth of his poetic talents, Crane considered himself 'healed, original now, and pure...' All his rich language and allusions to a world inherited from his affinities with the Elizabethan poets flooded back as he collided with his theme in an act of dionysian over-reach at which he excelled.

But no matter his return to poetry, and the high esteem in which Peggy held his latest creation, writing to her husband on 27 January that, 'he is by no means finished. It is a magnificent piece of lyric poetry that is built with the rhetorical splendour of a Dante in hell,' the poem's execution wasn't sufficient to re-establish a working rhythm in the irrevocably bibulous poet. Strung out by the anxieties connected with having disgraced the Guggenheim by reports of his drunken behaviour in Mexico, by the imminent financial crash of his father's estate, and by the equally intolerable state of sexual confusion created by his fling with Peggy, Crane began to disintegrate in the weeks leading up to his suicide. He made a half-hearted attempt to kill himself by drinking iodine, an offence that the doctor summoned had to officially report, thereby placing Crane under threat of deportation.

Investigating options for their return to New York, and given Hart's love of the sea and ships, the couple secured berths on the Orizaba, where it quickly became clear to Peggy that Crane's reputation was common knowledge amongst the uniformed crew. That Crane had made a number of the men was obvious, and when the Orizaba stopped off at Havana for six hours, Crane in becoming separated from Peggy, and in failing to keep their rendezvous at a café called the Diana, went off on a solitary binge with a sailor.

When Peggy anxiously returned to the ship, Crane she was told by the captain was already on board, and drinking in the bar. Disappointed by his behaviour, and additionally so in that she had purchased him the gift of a number of new records in Havana, Peggy went to the bar to look for him. Not finding him there, she ordered a cocktail, put on a record and lit a cigarette, only to have the box of Cuban matches explode in a violent flare that scorched her wrist and arm. Blacking out from the pain, she was carried to the surgery to have her arm treated with a solution of tannic acid. It was there, while she was being treated by the ship's surgeon, Richard Newman, that a belligerently disruptive Hart appeared, interrupting Newman's work and loudly threatening to sue the Ward Line itself. Ordered out by the doctor, Crane stayed on outside, and attempted to escort Peggy back to her cabin. Ordered to take a sleeping pill and go to bed, Peggy's rest was periodically interrupted by the distressed figure of the poet forcing his way into her cabin to continue his confused, self-accusing monologue laced with a drunk's recriminations against everything and everyone.

It was Crane's last stand. He was sailing back to a city that offered him no expectations, and no future. His ideal of the poet as visionary had been disowned by a society in which he had no place. At some stage in the night Crane was forcibly restrained and locked in his cabin, only to break out and go on a rampage in the sailors' quarters that resulted in him being badly beaten, before attempting to climb the ship's rail, and being wrestled to the deck by the watch at 3:30 a.m.

When Crane resurfaced at 10a.m., the steward reported that he was drinking copiously from a bottle of whisky. Dishevelled and nursing a black eye, he found his way to Peggy's cabin an hour later, and contritely confessed that his ring and wallet were missing, and that he had no memory of the previous night. Still in his pyjamas and a light topcoat, she persuaded him to eat a large breakfast of grapefruit, cereal, eggs and bacon and toast. Advising him he would feel better after he was shaved and dressed, Peggy did her best to persuade him to return to his cabin and put on clean clothes. 'I'm not going to make it dear. I'm utterly disgraced,' he told her, before leaving the room.

A few minutes later, and shortly before noon, Crane reappeared on deck. A large number of the Orizaba's ninety passengers who were assembled waiting for the results of the ship's pool watched Crane walk rapidly towards the stern. In the words of an eye-witness, 'He walked to the railing, took off his coat, folded it neatly over the railing (not dropping it on the deck), placed both hands on the railing, raised himself on his toes, and then dropped back again. We all fell silent and watched him wondering what in the world he was up to. Then, suddenly, he vaulted over the railing and jumped into the sea…'

Hart's drop into the ship's detonative wake, in waters policed by cruising sharks, 275 miles out of Havana, didn't however result in instant death. The same witness running to the rail, reported, 'Just once I saw Crane, swimming strongly, but never again. It was a scene I am unable to forget.' Either sucked under by the explosive churn of the ship's four-turbine engines, or lacerated by killer sharks, the four lifeboats lowered for rescue found no sight of Crane's body over a diligent two hour search. By the early afternoon the ship's captain, James Blackadder, was forced to conclude, 'If the propellors didn't grind him to mincemeat, then the sharks got him immediately.'

Crane died with the same intensity with which he had lived. Unconventional, uncompromising, he maintained his visionary belief to the last impacted second. More than any other writer of his generation he believed in living poetry to the full, not as an occasional practitioner, but as the total embodiment of the romantic ideal. If as Peggy Cowley commented, he had no other credential in life but his gift, then his death may be seen as a courageous defence of a talent that he considered worth taking into the ocean, rather than have it degraded by financial humiliation and the jobless future he faced. Crane literally disappeared into the blue, on a day when the Caribbean was the serene colour of lapislazuli, and with the ship riding the Tropic of Cancer. He leap was like a rifle crack. A clean whistle into the bottomless deeps.

heavens gate

Rancho Santa Fe in California is one of the wealthiest communities in the U.S. Positioned on the northern rim of San Diego, just 100 miles south of Los Angeles, Rancho Santa Fe has been a prestigious area for the privileged since the 1920s Hollywood gold rush. The enclosed enclave rarely has property for let as all of the home owners take full advantage of the status such a location provides. However in October 1996, an Iranian "businessman," Sam Koutchesfahani (sentenced in 1998 for tax evasion and visa fraud, later found to be connected to at least two of the September 11 terrorists), happened to have a vacant little $1.2 million number at 18241 Colina Norte, Rancho Santa Fe, just itching to be leased. Nothing ostentatious – 9,200 square feet perched on a three-acre lot with seven bedrooms, nine baths, a swimming pool, spa and tennis courts. Koutchesfahani had been trying unsuccessfully to sell the property when, luckily for Sam, the ideal tenants arrived offering to pay the $7,000/month rent in cash (music to a tax evader's ears).

According to Milton Silverman, Koutchesfahani's attorney, the tenants presented themselves as Christian-based angels sent to earth. The leader was a 66- year-old man introduced as Father John who told Koutchesfahani that they came from the Midwest and didn't believe the government should have any authority over them. In fact, the angels were a neo-Christian-New-Age-UFO cult named Heaven's Gate and "Father John," also known as Do (pronounced Doe), was their impish, twinkle-eyed charismatic leader born Marshall Herff Applewhite. They claimed to have no Social Security numbers and didn't use

129

bank accounts. Aside from their religious beliefs which often inclined towards Sci Fi fantasy, their strictly regimented lives were centered entirely on their work which involved computers and Web design. They operated a Web service called Higher Source that designed commercial home pages. Owning such a business provided them the anonymity and insularity they needed to conceal their peculiar lifestyle and rescue them from probing questions posed by the unenlightened. If there's one thing cults don't like, it's questions. Web design proved to be the perfect occupation to facilitate these true believers' retreat from the real world, abandoning all mental equilibrium and descending into an entirely subjective universe dictated by the neuroses of their leader Applewhite. Like the proverbial Big Brother monitor, Applewhite in paranoid anxiety supervised the lives of his flock. Koutchesfahani last saw the tenants on Sunday, March 23 when they, not so surprisingly, offered him one of their computers as a gift for one of his children.

On March 26 at 1:35 p.m. a San Diego 911 dispatcher received an anonymous tip that a mass suicide occurred at 18241 Colina Norta. The caller was Heaven's Gate escapee Rio D'Angelo, born Richard Ford, also known under his Heaven's Gate moniker Neody, who received a Federal Express package sent to him in Los Angeles containing a letter and two videotapes. The video tapes contained what appeared to be farewell messages from all of the Heaven's Gate members. They delivered their presentations in pairs, as they were instructed to live their lives, and all looked as if they had no qualms whatsoever about their impending fate. They were very cheerful and unrestrained about the whole event, any visible tears were tears of joy. The leader, Marshall Applewhite, was also documented in a grotesque performance of forced wide-eyed innocence and sincerity. Speaking in a supercilious measured manner, he said the members would be "shedding their containers" and "leaving this planet" then added, "You can follow us but you cannot stay here."

Finally, he urged viewers to "follow quickly." One could almost envision a demented children's television show host ushering the kiddies to their doom. This same care package was delivered to other recipients around the U.S. with a lengthy document enclosed stating, "By the time you read this we'll be gone – several dozen of us. We came from the Level of Above Human in distant space and we have now exited the bodies that we were wearing for our earthly task, to return to the world from whence we came – task completed."

Rio's employer, Nick Matzorkis, was initially skeptical when his employee expressed concern to him after watching the videos, so he offered to drive Rio himself to the Rancho Santa Fe mansion. Rio entered the house, found the bodies and emerged "white as a sheet" according to Matzorkis. Rio told his employer, "They did it." When Matzorkis asked, "Did what?" Rio replied, "They left their containers, they committed suicide."

One of the first two deputies to arrive at the suicide scene, Deputy Sheriff Robert Brunk, reported that before even entering the house he could smell a noxious odor emitting from the air conditioner that was left running. It was a smell he recognized as being produced by decaying bodies. After he and his partner found the first ten bodies, they returned outside, concerned for their own safety, and called for reinforcement. Ultimately, 39 cadavers in varying stages of decomposition were discovered in an immaculately clean dwelling. This was neither the blood bath nor the scene of carnage one might expect when answering an anonymous tip about a mass suicide. Remarkably, there wasn't a trace of disorder, chaos, confusion or panic detected.

On the contrary, the rooms were antiseptically clean and the corpses were resting as neatly as if they'd already been filed away in the county morgue. The first deputies to arrive described the scene as "calm" and "serene." Each carcass lay tidily atop freshly made bunk beds all lined up like UFO barracks. All were dressed in identical black sports clothes adorned with "Away Team" patches made especially for the occasion. They wore identical Nike brand sports shoes. Purple fabric cloths measuring 3-foot by 3-foot folded over into triangles covered their heads and chests. Cups of liquid mixtures sat nearby and eyeglasses were placed adjacent to the bodies. Small bags were carefully placed each bearing driver's licenses, passports and/or birth certificates of the corpses as if to aid the authorities – or someone – in identifying them. Inside the jacket pockets, the same amount of cash consisting of a $5 bill and some quarters was found. These provisions were ostensibly for their journey toward the "level beyond human," a journey believed to be expedited by the Hale-Bopp Comet passing through at that time.

The only three bodies to deviate from the uniformity of the others were two who had white plastic bags wrapped tightly around their heads and one who had a painter's mask over her head rather than the purple shrouds that her companions wore. These three individuals were thought to have been the last group to die. The same type of white plastic bags found wrapped around the heads of the two members were also discovered in the trash behind the house making it apparent that the bags had been used by everyone in the suicide mission. Presumably the last Away Teamers simply didn't have anyone left to remove their own bags and tidy up after them. This brought the body total to 21 women and 18 men. Brunk told his fellow officer, as they surveyed room after room of orderly abandoned corpses, "The next thing we do will bring the whole world in on us. You just don't get this kind of call every day." As it turned out, these two deputies had a close encounter with the largest mass suicide in U.S. history.

Tattered recipes were found in the trash suggesting that members mix bites of pudding or applesauce with drugs, then swallow a vodka mixture and lie back to die. The lethal formula consisted of mixing phenobarbital, applesauce or pudding, and vodka. The barbiturate phenobarbital, when ingested in large quantity and combined with alcohol, produces a swift coma-like effect. Autopsies revealed that anywhere between two milligrams (non-lethal) and eleven grams (exceedingly lethal) of the barbiturate were detected in their blood streams. Technically the lethal dose would be six grams. A variation of this barbiturate/alcohol formula is found in Derek Humphrey's notorious book *Final Exit* which provides instructions on various means of suicide.

Inside the house, investigators found a document that shed some light on the way the suicides were organized. Judging by the degree of decomposition of the bodies upon discovery, it was apparent that the suicides occurred at various times over about a three day period. Labeled "The Routine," the document outlined a process by which the first group of 15 people would kill themselves, assisted by eight other people. Then a second group of 15 would commit suicide, assisted by eight people. Given that 39 victims were found, that would have left a final group of nine. By the time the cyclical routine dwindled down to the last three disciples, Judith Ann Rowland, Susan Francis Strom, and Julie Elmira LaMontagne, a new variation of the suicide cocktail was utilized to beam them up to the level above human. Lab reports indicate that the lethal mixture ingested by the last three to die also included a strong opiate painkiller, hydrocodone, in addition to the phenobarbital and alcohol. Aside from these last members, only the leader, Applewhite tested positive for hydrocodone. Of the last three members to go, it is speculated that Rowland was the final death since the other two were suffocated with white plastic bags tied tightly with elastic strings and she was not; instead Rowland was found with only a painter's mask covering her face, most likely to screen the putrid gases of her Away Team buddies who had already shed their containers.

Judith Ann found herself utterly alone. No classmates left with whom to watch *Star Trek Voyager*, *Deep Space Nine*, *X-Files* or

Straight to hell

Millennium (the approved television shows for the Away Team). Nobody to share Heaven's Gate authorized communal cuisine of KFC extra crispy family meal, topping it off with Starbucks JavaChip ice cream and a lemonade, cayenne pepper and maple syrup "master cleanser" chaser. No more PC Games with her classmates. And never again would she know what to do on her own anymore for she'd been trained to believe that she must be suspicious of even her own judgment. Anyone else might at least have a fleeting thought to bolt and begin a new life; who cares if her fellow space cadets tsked at her from above? Instead, Rowland obediently boarded the Hale-Bopp comet to go up, up and Away Team and was indeed among the 39 to die.

Considering their obsession with UFOs and space travel, Heaven's Gate must have felt they had quite a trophy ambassador for the level above human with one certain long-standing member. Among the dead was Thomas Nichols, brother of Nichelle Nichols, the actress who played Lt. Uhura in the original "Star Trek" series. In an interview on CNN's "Larry King Live" shortly after the suicides, Nichelle Nichols said her 58-year-old brother had been a member of the group for about twenty years and that he had very little contact with his family during that time. Nichols added that several years before his death, her brother and some other Heaven's Gate members contacted her for suggestions as to the best way of spreading their message to the public. She said, "[They] asked me what I thought would be the best way to let the world know what they were about...They talked about the great comet that would come some day."

Beneath the cheery exterior, Heaven's Gate messiah Do, or Marshall Applewhite was intensely misanthropic. He suffered from confused sexual signals and a furious need for validation. Like many cult leaders, he tried to channel his shortcomings into a synthesized philosophy-religion promoting the idea of a utopian existence somewhere other than the material world of horrors. Applewhite harvested the respect he so coveted by lovingly teaching all his followers to be virtual clones of himself. Androgyny was the key in appearance and behavior and the group all followed Do's lead. Both male and female members of the group affected a unisex look, with buzz-cut hair styles and shapeless, sexless clothes. Their appearance caused investigators at first to mistakenly identify all of the bodies as young men when actually most were women. Applewhite demanded that all Heaven's Gate members practice celibacy, as did he. According to the suicide autopsy reports, many of the male disciples astonishingly sacrificed their testes in veneration of their castrated leader.

Among Do's other teachings was the classic cult specialty of developing disdain for anyone outside of the Heaven's Gate commune. Do flattered his would-be alien flock that they were an elite elect far superior to the non-initiated humans whom he considered to be deluded zombies. Early in Applewhite's career as space-cult mentor, he became sensitive to the idea that outsiders might think he'd lost his marbles. He commented to follower Sharon Walsh, "by social, psychiatric, medical and religious standards we...have long since lost our sanity." Applewhite effectively fed this paranoid persecution complex to his followers to ensure blind loyalty to the group and himself while fostering alienation from the mundane world. This paradoxical superior/fearful attitude towards "Them" (i.e., anyone who is not one of "Us") is one of the simplest means of hooking even the most skeptical curiosity seeker into the solipsistic netherworld of a leader's insecure and threatened worldview.

Like many a cult guru, Applewhite believed that he "just wasn't made for this world." One could describe him as someone who had severed his connections with objectivity altogether, existing in a universe of his own unique perceptions. As a result, he had no more use for logic. After all, in a universe based entirely on his own neuroses, everything is exactly as he desired it to be. He might have even believed himself to be god or the universe itself. Obviously to his small number of followers he was just that.

Yet, even today one can find information on the Internet from the last surviving Heaven's Gate member, Rio D'Angelo, a.k.a. Neody, who first discovered the bodies, and who still carries the torch for Applewhite, rationalizing the actions of his deceased classmates. "They weren't trying to kill themselves because of a crazy idea, although some people saw it as a crazy idea," DiAngelo says. "It really is an advanced level of being." Never a shortage of true believers.

mark rothko

"If I choose to commit suicide, everyone will be sure of it.
There will be no doubts" – Rothko

In London's Tate Modern gallery, is a room devoted to the work
of the Russian born artist Mark Rothko. A room without
windows, without a view, no portal to signs of outer space or the
passage of outer time. On the walls are six large paintings, related
in colour (mostly dark maroon, with red overlays and black ...
spilt wine, dried blood) each one the size of a domestic room's
wall. In such a smaller room, the experience of surrender to them
would be interlaced with a deeper, darker foreboding,
apprehension of entrapment, enforced containment. Framed
spaces large enough to engulf you, an enforced embrace, yet at
the same time seeming to en-courage (en-power) you to float out
of time and space completely. Capitulate to the infinite. *Le gout de
l'infini.* A tension between absence and presence that threatens,
offering an aching insight into the anguish and pain of Rothko's
all-too tangibly bedevilled vision of the world within. Within
these seductive spaces, the imagination is at its outer limits, soft-
edged, floating, formless. shimmering. Some might say: colour
and texture reduced to pure spirit.

This large room with its six paintings is probably the closest
example of a Rothko chapel in Houston. A more than half-decent
equivalent for we Londoners, in which to garner some faith in the
face of a world of commodities, and dying hope. Sit in the room
within the room, half close the eyes and the paintings become
carpets, magic carpets, sacred spaces, images shored up against
Osirian fragmentation, delineated by mere brush stokes, mostly
rendered invisible in the sombre, imperturbable light. Spaces in

which, on which, through which, the mind attempts to focus on infinity and yet, not unwillingly, accepts defeat; accepts the pleasure of the pure aesthetic, the subtle and tantalising beauty that reminds us of feeling, rekindles emotion, a sense of the flesh we only temporarily, vicariously inhabit; beyond sensations, the inner dream webs of Being, dying, cassation, the mind fading at the edges, losing memories, fearing dreams; dissolving the hard-edged frames that are the load-bearing structure of the prison house of reason. Each rectangular painting, a grave.

London has these six paintings, not by mere chance but by good fortune.

The paintings were originally commissioned in the late 50's for the walls of the very fashionable Four Seasons Restaurant in the magnificent architectural masterpiece, the Seagram building on New York's Park Avenue. Rothko built huge scaffold structures in his studio, from which he could paint the images, creating the exact dimensions of the restaurant, the whole project inspired, he said, by Michelangelo's murals for the Laurentian Library in Florence, where the window spaces are deliberately blinded; the interior suffused with uneasy melancholy. Rothko said Michelangelo had achieved exactly the feeling he was looking for, which he hoped to recreate, making the viewers feel they were "trapped in a room where all the doors and windows are bricked up, so that all they can do is butt their heads forever against the wall". The word "forever" is more than ominous ...

But something was calling Rothko from within, and rather than the bright and more colourful images of his earlier work, despite himself, the paintings demanded their own life and spirit, and came out darker than anything he had painted before. Reluctantly, he recognised the images were completely unsuitable for a classy, chic restaurant – people eating caviar and chatting stock market prices and worldly nonsense – and withdrew from the commission.

Rothko had always considered J M Turner to be a profound inspiration, especially in his own earlier work. He had almost certainly seen single, large gallery rooms devoted entirely to this one artist, to the later almost abstract Turner seascapes, as if they too had been painted as murals in a single inter-connected vision; so he presented the set of paintings to the Tate Gallery, to show his affection for England and its artists, and the first time they were hung together in the Tate, Rothko was there to supervise. The space was compact, the light reduced, so that the subtle layered surfaces, each relating to the other, presented a brooding ambience, demanding contemplation. Stillness. Uncertainty. Doubt ...

The murals, painted with oil on canvas in 1958 or 1959, each with either black or red on maroon, bestow a variety of invitations to escape from the self. The largest painting seems to have a floating door in its centre, like an Egyptian temple door (always fake, painted to resemble a real door). The shape floating on the darkest of the taller paintings curiously seems to suggest the stone pillars of Stonehenge. Another has an inner shape that conjures up a double window, opening upon nothing ... the faint hint of preternatural light, in wash of colour floating down. Each painting is an implied orifice, a call to the womb, to a highly seductive and yet threatening inner contained space and night ... death and imminent birth in a terrible embrace.

The words of Tim Buckley's *Song To The Siren* ... "Death my bride, I'm as puzzled as the new born babe ... " would seem an ideal caption. As the murals would also be an appropriate setting for Mozart's *The Magic Flute* ... the Temple devoted to Isis and her dismembered lover, Osiris. Or the grottos in which Gerard de Nerval imagined he too had soared and fallen with the sirens: "J'ai revé les grottes ou nagent les sirènes ... "

How could a man, a once poor man now rich and celebrated around the world, who could create such sublime minimalist beauty, die such a savage bloody death at his own hand? But as Sylvia Plath foresaw and foretold – a warning no artist can ignore – that dying is an art, just as art is a permanent, untiring, relentless adversary, whose hidden agenda is always a continuous practice at dying, continuous fraught initiations into the mysteries of the Angel of Death. She is the muse ... Rothko dared to warn us of such enigmas, the conflict between sensuality and spirit, in all his work, but then gave us the revelation of its deepest anguish, the proof beyond any denial, in his death, at his own hand. As a solace, he offered us moments of peace on the Way. Go to the Tate Rothko temple and dare to imagine your own death, as you recall Rothko's final ritual in the sensual arms of his imagined siren bride.

Take a train south from St. Petersburg and you arrive in Dvinsk. It is now called Daugavpils. Once, its people were largely Jews. Its heart was devoted to commerce. And *Les Fleurs du Mal.* Many of the poorer pretty young Jewish girls were forced to choose prostitution to survive. It was not difficult to perceive many valid reasons, under savage Russian military oppression, for families of the better-off Jews to dream of immigration. Rothko's mother was sixteen when she married. Her son, Marcus Rothkowitz was a late child, the youngest of four, enveloped from birth in the seductive dream of ultimate, if not infinite, freedom; by means of the escape to England: or America.

Rothko was eleven when his father died. Freud would write that the death of the father inflicts a terrible psychic burden on a son – the most dangerous age for the death to occur is around the age of eleven. At the age of nine, though, Rothko had (vicariously as it would turnout) denounced his father's traditional ways, announced that he would no longer attend the family's local Jewish temple; with the family. You might say he had killed his father a couple of years before his father really died; ultimately assuming within himself a supreme sense of power, albeit forever undermined by guilt. The youngest son (eight years younger than his brother), the sensitive and hypochondriac favourite of his mother, he had been blessed (and cursed) by achieving his unconscious incestuous goal ... through the death of the father, full possession of her. Thus his doomed passion for the oceanic, *le mer, la mère*, had begun ...

Rotho's paintings are screens in which liquid (oil colour) floats, temporarily arrested in time, restless, moon- and tide-driven seascapes; crystalline structures (and non-structures) trapped on the verge of lattice formulation or dissolution, poised at the tantalising threshold of melting or crystallising as witnessed on a translucent glass microscope slide; ideally, under polarising light.

Hard at the edges (he had killed his father) and soft at the centre (he had won his mother), this Oedipal son would live all his life with the sphinx's smile taunting his dreams, a tortured painter who wanted most of all to escape the pain of light, the father's domain, light as power, sexual power, the permanent predicament of seeing, or being seen; omnipotence or dismemberment; the project of becoming blind, but gifted with clairvoyance and insight, like Tiresias: always the adversary and yet redeemer of Oedipus. In his work, Rothko seems to be desperately trying to deny the very existence of that real, sun-lit father's world; he would see nothing of that real world but everything in a lunar mindscape reminiscent of a fellow Russians vision, Tarkovsky – as in *Solaris,* or *Stalker.* It would not have been a surprise if Rothko had painted all his work as variations on the theme of the colour violet ...

And so it was that Rothko, despite every success and all the recognition he might have imagined he needed, after creating temples in which his murdered father's spirit might be deemed to promise him forgiveness, he was finally forced to give up the struggle to maintain harmony over his inner chaos (denied in his harmonious musical paintings). At the violet hour he murdered himself – murdered the father in himself (at a late age he had fathered a child with a much younger wife, much to his own and everyone's surprise) – as brutally as he was capable.

His paintings are an evolving, meandering record of his perpetual confrontation with a death desired, at the arterial heart's crossroads. Murder of his other, guilty self; the self that had could only see, eventually, as false, fake, inauthentic. There was no going back to innocence; there never is, after the father is murdered at the crossroads.

It seems almost churlish to mention it: mere names resonating oddly, but Borges would surely celebrate the parallels. In Edgar Allen Poe's most prestigious short story(many say his most profound expression of the inward windings and secret aspects of

his own creative process). The writer of fictions which are
nevertheless true; and yet are also not true? In the story entitled
"The Purloined Letter" the principle character is the Detective
Dupin. It is Dupin who toils at the mystery and finally, with weird
Tiresian insight, reveals the esoteric truth behind a somewhat
symbolic theft of a letter, a theft which enables the commitment
of a number of more serious crimes, summed up in the phrase:
"The ascendency depended on the robber's knowledge of the
loser's knowledge of the robber."

The detective brought in to investigate the death and
apparent paradoxes of Rothko's suicide, was a certain Detective
Lappin.

Rothko killed himself in the early morning of February 25th,
1970; alone in his 69th street studio. His assistant found him and
ran to a neighbour to say: "I think Mr. Rothko is very sick." A
terrible understatement, as the artist was lying spread-eagled on
his back as if crucified in a huge pool of dried blood. Another
assistant, Frank Ventgen was called and saw immediately that
Rothko was dead. Two policeman assumed a suicide, but called
on Detective Lappin to verify the facts. At the time, the fabled
detective was being accompanied in his work by a newspaper
reporter, Paul Wilkes, writing a story with the odd working title:
"Why so many Real-Life Detective Stories End with a Rubber
Stamp". Lappin at the time was reading Puzo's *The Godfather*.

The first description of Rothko's suicide, taken from the
detective's brash account, turned out to be wrong in important
details. He described the body lying in a pool of blood, the water
in the sink still running. To save the people who found the body
the trouble of cleaning up! Lappin sees the razor blade with
kleenex tissue attached to it and comments, somewhat laconically,
that suicides invariably try not to cut their fingers when cutting
their wrists. Rothko's trousers were neatly folded over the back of
a chair. Lappin decides he didn't want to get blood on them:
cutting his wrists at the sink, he fell back to the floor when the
blood levels got too low. Lappin seemed full of certainty, even
noticing a number of small "hesitant cuts" on the forearm,
declaring them as trials of the sharpness of the blade.

Lappin calls the artist's doctor who confirms he was depressed after a recent operation, his health generally bad. Lappin declares with the certainty of one who was there at the time: "An open-and-shut suicide".

But the story of Rothko's death was already metamorphosing into fiction. He had not had a recent operation and there was only one hesitation cut. The journalistic account (Wilkes wasn't there when the body was found) became more than current gossip but the gospel truth, so much so that the artist Robert Motherwell pronounced he was surprised, on hearing the story, that the suicide had been so ritualistic. The story people heard and later read, was purloined by an opportunist journalist from the Detective Lappin's fanciful pulp-fiction version of the events, mostly speculations of his own invention; especially as he had never heard of Rothko, and must have surveyed the huge abstract paintings around the studio as proof of the poor man's unbalanced mind.

The police examiners decided that Rothko had taken a huge dose of barbiturates before killing himself. Later official autopsy found that Rothko had a "marked senile emphysema" and advanced heart disease, and did not have long to live. There were two cuts that caused the death, one 2 and a half inches long and a half inch deep on the left arm, and one 2 inch long and 1 inch deep on his right arm, deep enough to almost sever the brachial artery. The report misspelt his name as Rothknow; and the corpse was numbered #1867. Official police versions, taped and never transcribed, depended mostly on Lappin's street-cred assumptions.

Rothko had taken a large dose of a drug, Sinequan, prescribed to him by his psychiatrist Dr. Klein, presumably to numb some of the pain, but mostly, his perceptions of his actions. He took off his shoes and suit, laying his trousers over the back of the chair. He made the cut in his left arm first, and the deeper one in the right. He was lying on his back, when found, in a pool of blood six foot by eight foot; with his "arms outstretched".

Rothko had often talked of suicide and written about it. He'd told his assistant Ahearn, "If I choose to commit suicide, everyone will be sure of it. There will be no doubts ... " He often referred to the "accidental deaths" of Jackson Pollock and David Smith, both drunk and killed by crashing their cars. Clearly forms of subliminal suicide. And despite the severity of his own illnesses, he continued to smoke and drink, aware that he was hastening his own death.

Recent separation from his wife and very young son, together with the knowledge of the imminence of a natural death from his failing health, Rothko chose the death that he could be utterly sure of, a theft of what time remained of his life. He wanted a death framed in his own space and time, his own hands, determined to make it conscious, utterly tangible and known, every detail under his control, robbed it of its uncertainty. Made it his own creation. He defeated God as he had defeated his own father. A solitary death, a singular vision, unseen, which now can only be imagined by us.

One of Rothko's friends wanted to take a photograph of the body lying in its pool of congealed blood, but he was persuaded not to, and so we are fortunately spared the theft of this painfully real image, which would surely have always clouded our perceptions of his paintings ... would we not see his body, crucified, hovering on the surface of every canvas? Unsullied by the pagan facts of his self-murder, we are left with blameless images of his paintings, striving towards transcendence of the real, the body, the flesh, the callous impersonality and decay of the material world: each painting a tentative, barely perceptible step towards the final blood-letting, in which his congealed blood, bone-dry on the concrete harsh floor, would surely have suggested the surfaces and colourings of the red and black on maroon canvasses hanging, forever, for us, in the Tate Modern.

thomas hamilton

From the introduction to *Dunblane: Our Year Of Tears* by Peter Samson and Alan Crow (Mainstream, Edinburgh, 1997):

His name is not worthy of appearing in print alongside those men, women and children who were affected by his wanton destruction. Quite simply, he has no place in this story of courage and hope.

From *The European*, issue 305, 14-20 March 1996. "The Massacre Of The Innocents" by Askold Krushelnycky and Julie Read:

A lone gunman, armed with four handguns, stormed into the gym of a Scottish primary school just after pupils had arrived on the morning of 13 March and opened fire.

Fifteen children and their teacher died in the gym while another child died in hospital. The killer apparently committed suicide by turning one of his weapons on himself.

Up to 17 other children were injured from the first-form class of four- and five-year-old boys and girls. Some were seriously wounded and underwent emergency surgery.

Hamilton was chased away from a school by outraged idiot parents acting on their smug suspicions. Only. Years before he went into the school at Dunblane and murdered sixteen very young children and just one teacher. There is the possibility that he went to the school planning to shoot up the assembly rather than the gymnasium. The morning assembly having ended ten minutes earlier than usual that morning. That he was actually looking for more teachers than kids. It's possible that he panicked having gone there with all his guns and knowing that it was all over anyway.

You've stalled.

You know what a creep really is? How they act? What they're looking for? Constantly. What little they're constantly fucking looking for? You expect them to be grateful, don't you? But they never are.

The *Chicago Tribune* summed it, and him, up in two out of only three paragraphs on May 20, 1996 underneath the headline "Children's Killer Quietly Cremated":

Thomas Hamilton, the vengeful misfit who massacred 16 children and their teacher at a Scottish school, was cremated Tuesday in a secret family service. Six days after his murderous rampage and suicide, the ceremony took place well away from Dunblane, the Scottish town he plunged into grief, police said. Only his family was present.

Kent Klich, a moody photographer who's published excellent studies of a heroin addicted prostitute (*The Book Of Beth*, Aperture, NY, 1989) and glued up Mexican street children (*El Nino*, Syracuse, NY, 1998) released *Children Of Ceausescu* (Umbridge, NY) in 2001. The Romanian children he photographed for it, from 1994 to 1999, were almost all infected with AIDS. And, unlike Raymond Depardon's very similar *Silence Rompu*, Klich's book does include some brief text on the delayed fate of the children lovingly captured in sad big-eyed black and white. Tacky brief explanations made worse by being sectioned into triptych: Family Life, Orphanage Life and New Beginnings. Altruistic gluttony; insulting only to the artist and his admirers. One particular set of before and after shots of a little one living with extreme facial scars from a wart condition so thick on her face as to almost completely obliterate it is virtually unviewable.

That brutal non-sexual sadness does not carry over to the

shots that the morning newspaper detailers have robbed of their faces. The obscured photos of children chained to beds and shackled to walls that were fed to the media in the wake of The Wonderland arrest publicity campaign. These censored kiddie porn stills were picked to deliver maximum shock but were disappointing because of their simple-minded utilitarianism. The frozen frames were lone portraits. Children made to pose. Before. Or without. A single adult appendage touching them. Condom'd vulgarity. A simple advertising construct. Mike Echols, an anti-child porn crusader who died in prison awaiting a hearing on indecent exposure charges, used to feature stills from child pornography on his website with the, mostly boys', faces intact but their genitals blacked out. He used to fib that his interest was in educating the public as to how bad the material really is. As well as assisting in the possible identification of the naked children: Presumed missing and always in danger. It was Echol's name that worked as a password for entry into a notorious child pornography website for years before he finally died. He also gained infamy among web browsers who used his name as a successful search word through legitimate servers to locate other providers and links in much the same way as Pete Townshend used "Russian Orphanages" and "Boys".

A year after the massacre in Dunblane, Eileen Harrild cried when she told the authors of a book on the shootings about how she hid in a storeroom with bleeding children. She had been shot in the chest, arm and hand. She recalled that one little boy lay next to her and whispered:

"What a bad man, what a bad man."

The same book captured the difficulties of little boy victim Coll Austin, now blind and deaf on one side only. Coll's father told the authors that Coll remembers Hamilton and the details of the shooting:

straight to hell

"Sometimes he gets very irritated. If he spills a drink on his blind side he says that it's HIS fault. He says: 'It's his fault I spilled my drink because I can't see properly.'"

The authors of this book, Peter Samson and Alan Crow (*Dunblane: Our Year Of Tears,* Mainstream Publishing, 1997) refused to put Thomas Hamilton's name on any page.

This is how you give a blow-job. You have to learn how to suck so that they feel it. How to lick it and, most importantly, how to respond back to the pleasure that you're giving. So that you can surprise and excite the owner of the cock even more. So that he'll cum just exactly like you want to. Maybe he'll want to do it again with you. Maybe he'll appreciate, simply, what you've just done. Maybe he'll think differently of you.

Just watch. Think that could be you. Sucking that cock. Doing that well and not caring anyways. Like watching a father cry on tv. About his little 7-year-old son found raped and murdered and dumped in the Vermillion River in Streator, Illinois. There's lumpen cocksuckers out there who want their straight trade to hate their needy girlishness. Men who want a taste of smelly cock and then expect to get beat up afterwards. If not, during.

What is it about having a cock grow hard in your mouth, by technique, or having it exposed to you, no matter what you are at that moment, that excites you? What do you want out of the experience? Immediately. Most faggot cocksuckers find the choking subservience that women spit back into themselves to be a little too tacky. But then their constant itching doesn't quite speak to the opposite.

What is the defining characteristic of your obsession with sex. Is it your ugliness or your lack of shame. And what came to the top first. Which one followed.

What convinced the hog to bundle in after he got sick of

masturbating at home all alone. What big little mistake led him to believe that the tiny orgasm he had just completed wouldn't suffer the same sudden drop-off if it came with a real bag of kneaded flesh. Why hasn't he come to his senses. Why hasn't he already given up. What makes him think there's something better anywhere other than his personality defects.

Thomas Watt Hamilton would've been all porky cock in his porn proclivities. You don't find balding bespectacled dorks in the photos posted in the members sections looking for hook-ups. Just their cocks. In mirrors or shot straight down, sat flat. Erect if small or average. Half-hard usually, no matter what. Judging from his loneliness and body type. And I've looked all over for porn shots of uncut cocks that might be thick and small Scottish like his could have been. Last time I was in London – as close as I got to Scotland – I searched for old men his age and temperament. Went to the irritating haunts I figured fat lonely gay men who liked skinny young boys would go and tried, badly, to make those connections.

I still wanted an old man. A selfish rank old fatting rat. Who could not control himself. Who's buckled under. Who doesn't know he gave up.

The popular history of Thomas Hamilton is left to the incompetent hands of any number of his victim's parents. The picayune rutting details that crammed his ugly lonely troll's life are seen as unnecessary and vulgar next to the importance of recognizing perpetual grief. The only two books on his case are both framed around the embers of the little or collective victim. Written as if their authors don't know what section of the bookstore their memorials will end up in. As if unaware of how web browsers will come across their names from now on.

Hamilton was only 22 when he was first fired from the Boy Scouts. The official reason was his ineptitude as a leader. But he knew it was because the assholes thought he was a pervert.

straight to hell

Decades later the dismissal still caused him trouble. He had operated his boysclubs and camps at a loss and had been unable to turn his dream into anything more than a hobby and a quest. And just before he walked into the gymnasium at Dunblane Primary School. And shot to death sixteen little children. Almost all of them only five years old. He had been rejected from putting an ad into an amateur photography magazine that would have been another chance at self-reliance. The magazine suspected that he might be dealing in stolen parts. Hamilton tried to think of ways of scratching a living out of his other interest; his handgun collection.

From "The Life And Death Of Thomas Hamilton" (Nick Cohen, *The Independent On Sunday*, March 17, 1996):

The boys whom he ordered to strip and run around in swimming trunks laughed at him behind his back and called him Mr. Creepy. The scores of adults he knew in Dunblane recognized weirdness and nicknamed him Spock. His podgy face and insinuating voice had made their flesh crawl, they said.

Even if they had not heard the rumours about Hamilton and his boys' camps which had been going on for 25 years, people in Dunblane suspected that something was wrong. And to his neighbors in Kent Road, Stirling, he stood out in the poor but friendly street as a man with little to say. George Smart said he had not got a word out of his neighbor in two years. He would see him walking by dressed in the classic nerd's anorak, head down, hands shoved into pockets.

And.

It is natural to assume that a mass child murderer with a long record of suspicious behavior and pictures of half-naked boys on his wall is also a paedophile. But it is possible that Hamilton was not a systematic child abuser; certainly he was never convicted.

Dave Norris, who knew Hamilton for 10 years, said he struck him as harmless. "It just seemed to me he wanted to give boys the childhood he never had. I couldn't believe it when I heard what this articulate educated man had done."

Remain objective. Lise Sarfati's lush color photographs of youthful boys and girls taken from separate centers for underaged delinquents in Russia. The naked, tall, hung young men shower themselves in Ikcha. And the naked young girls soak their fatty winter bodies from metal pans and bowls in Vyedyenski. It is impossible not to choose one over the other. To compare. To find the gender that is more wanting. The least reminiscent of a pack of bleached wet walruses. The boys are skinny and their heads are shaved like bathroom psychopaths. The women are comfortable and crowded. The boys alone and vulnerable.

Sophie North, pictured in color inside her father's book on her loss and the other murders in Dunblane, is a cute enough five-year-old. Her father has included these photos in his *Dunblane: Never Forget* (Mainstream, 2000) so that you could see the reality of Thomas Hamilton's pathetic rage. Pictures of her wide-eyed and smiling. She wears her Scot school uniform with its lovely compact skirt. She pets a kitty. Smiles up from a pillow. Stands in front of her birthday cake at her birthday party. She is an unspectacular child. And her death is all the more miserable, worthless and cruel because it came in a group of fifteen other children. And one adult. Her father dilutes his grief with anti-gun politics and british law changing campaigns. He doesn't see the little one the way his customers will. He can't convey what made her unique to him.

Hamilton didn't stuff one of the kids into a van to rape them before he died. Too. He didn't pull any special one out of the bloody runs and teams and try to find out what one so small would have tasted like before he committed suicide.

Sophie North's color photos are typical of any little girl that age. A photo of her at the beach, with her watchful father in the background, is nothing more than cute and homespun. The tragedy of her absence is not present in the snapshot.

Thomas Hamilton collected photos and videos of the boys he used to help as part of his boyscout contributions.

No sex. No pornography.

Robert Black, who raped and murdered little girls in the back of his van as he drove around England looking for single chances, had a substantial collection of child pornography in his apartment when arrested. He was obsessed with finding out how far his fingers could fit inside the little girls he murdered. He told a lazy book writer and a doctor all about it after his arrest. And they ate it whole.

There are no concrete details of Mr. Hamilton actually molesting any children. We only know that there was gossip and uncomfortable accusations. In fact, his earliest rejection by the Scouts was for suspicion of homosexuality. Not child molestation. And it was this unease that was never officially acknowledged but merely discussed and traded in private that continued to dog all of Hamilton's many efforts to get his kid's groups off the ground.

Mr. Hamilton had an extensive collection of photographs of the children that he had tried so hard to keep interested in his shoe-string scouting experiences. He insisted that the children conform to certain fetishistic dress requirements. He liked them skinny and shirtless and wearing oversized black shorts. Which a pedophile might think was due to a lovely chance, every now and again, of the little boys' balls flopping out next to the large space created by the billowing pant. Or he liked them tight and a size too small. He picked favorites among the boys. And ran his clubs in a militaristic fashion. Often worrying the parents with all his shouting.

There are important details contained in the extremely worthwhile *Public Inquiry Into The Shootings At Dunblane Primary School On 13 March 1996* by The Hon Lord Cullen:

Another matter which was of concern to parents was his practice of taking photographs of the boys posing in their black trunks while taking deep breaths, without the knowledge or permission of their parents. For this purpose he used not only a still camera but also a video camera which he acquired about 1989 and possessed for about five years. (...) The boys did not seem to be enjoying themselves but appeared silent and even frightened. There was also an over-concentration on parts of the boys' bodies, especially the naked upper parts along with long lingering shots of the area between the waist and knees.

And.

Concerns had also been raised about the nature of the photographs which he had taken and about a trip to an island where the children had been forced to take part in the making of a videofilm on the lines of "The Lord Of The Rings". In particular one child was forced to lie in cold water against his will. The children were cold and wet and were dressed only in swimming trunks during a rain shower as Thomas Hamilton prevented them from putting their clothes on. When he was asked to provide photographs he had taken Thomas Hamilton denied that he had taken any still photographs.

And.

One of the boys who was interviewed later said that he had been singled out by Thomas Hamilton, taken alone to an individual tent and photographed in red-coloured swimming trunks. DS Hughes feared that this boy was being singled out for special treatment and perhaps for future abuse. Thomas Hamilton denied any such intention and denied taking such photographs. (...) Among the photographs which were recovered there were a large number of the particular boy who was plainly a favourite and had been given special jobs in the camp. However, there were no photographs of him wearing red swimming trunks. (...) As regards the photographs which were recovered by the police, although there were various different poses by boys wearing black *swimming trunks there was no explicit indecency. DS Hughes considered that Thomas Hamilton had been untruthful about the photographs. The nature of them made him concerned about the "stability" of his personality and his unhealthy interest in children.*

It has been suggested that Hamilton was pushed to suicide and murder as an easily understood act of rage and revenge. Some local officials and loud parents had made his non-physical interest in boys absolutely impossible. He was branded a pervert before he was allowed to prove it. Hamilton may have killed the children to do nothing more than attack the parents. His method of murder by gun was his least physical option and – from the descriptions of little survivors who witnessed his singular sexless mind-set – this seems to have been the case. Hamilton was methodical in the only two to three minutes it took to spray the school's gymnasium with tiny sad blood. After the initial rampage, Hamilton merely shot the ones that didn't seem dead. It wasn't much of an orgy despite the possibilities. No rapes. No gropes. No phallic substitutes. No jerking off one last time. No acknowledgment of the little five-year-olds' fragile beauty.

Hamilton was not stopped before he did any damage.

There is a time when the poor old rube figured that was all he was ever going to be allowed. That whatever god had made him had forever consigned his possibilities to nothing more warmly real than looking and staring and coveting and cumming quietly onto a clasped forefinger and thumb above his clenched fist. And then wiping it into a kleenex. And flushing it down the toilet. And then having to hide the photographs that only hinted at eleven-year-old cock size and balls bulge and the thin boney trail that formed a cross between their pink nipples. Pointing down to the flat stomachs just above where their pubic thatches would someday grow out over their lengthening thickening soft hung dicks. Very important.

There are details and witness reports in The Cullen

Report that were proved false by a lack of "corroboration":

Secondly, another person, whose statement was read to the Inquiry, stated that when he was 12 years of age (in 1985) he attended Thomas Hamilton's club at Bannockburn. In the summer he was one of a party of eight boys who went to Loch Lomond with him and stayed in his cabin cruiser. He described an occasion when Thomas Hamilton in his cabin touched him between his legs and on his private parts; told him to lie face down on a bed where he started to push his fingers into his rectum and stroked his back. Thomas Hamilton's shorts were off and his penis erect. He then told him to face the side of the cabin and ran his hand up and down his back while breathing heavily. Up to that point Thomas Hamilton was striking him from time to time with a telescopic pointer.

The March 17th 1996 issue of *The News Of The World* featured an interview with Richard Young, a manager of a hostel in Edinburgh, who said that he rented rooms to Hamilton and a fourteen-year-old boy:

"He went up with the boy at around 11pm. I went to bed next door.
The doors are very thin. I could hear the boy whimpering."
Several weeks later Hamilton rang Young to say he was bringing a boy from the youth club he ran in Stirling.
"They stayed in the same room as before", he said. "I could hear them again."
Again Young let the chance of nailing the pervert go by.
The manager eventually asked two of Hamilton's "guests" what went on.
"They said he paid them 25 pounds each to strip off", he revealed. "Then they said he made them do things to each other. They told me he was taking lots of photographs throughout and later they all went to sleep in the same bed."

The *International Express* for 20 to 26 March, 1996, ran two 1989

straight to hell

shots of Hamilton being chased and attacked by angry mothers. Women who were sick of what they suspected Hamilton was carefully doing and getting away with. The article aimed wide: *More details of Hamilton's sordid sex fantasies also emerged. Detectives, investigating whether he had any links with known paedophile groups, already know that he tried to join a sex club in Edinburgh.*

When the club turned him down – too aggressive" – he threatened them, bombarding the club owner's girlfriend with obscene phone calls and threats. In his application to join the club balding podgy Hamilton described himself as 41 – he was 43 – blue-eyed, and muscular.

Hamilton begged to be dominated and beaten by prostitutes, and pestered the club to find a woman to have sex with him in the open air. He was particularly obsessed about videoing a couple having sex in a tent at one campsite where he ran outward-bound holidays for boys.

Police are also examining piles of video tapes found at his filthy council home. Local newsagents said he was a regular customer for porn.

From *The Independent On Sunday* from March 17, 1996:

By the early 1990's, photography shops in Stirling were refusing to develop Hamilton's pictures of boys at Loch Lomond. They said they were obscene, but the police said they were not obscene enough for a prosecution.

In 1992 Fife Council, which borders Dunblane, banned Hamilton from it's schools after concern about the films he was making of boys. Two more police inquiries were made in 1993. Central Regional Council warned teachers to contact its legal department before dealing with Hamilton. In 1994, he was cautioned by police after being caught behaving indecently with a young man in Edinburgh.

It's not likely that Thomas Hamilton went looking for a blow-job. Stop pretending that you went in looking for a suck. You didn't. Nobody does. But. You will find that these beasts moan and melt more than they ever managed to conceive once they find a receptive mouth. They don't know what they want because they're so sick on what little they get.

Edited by Jack Hunter

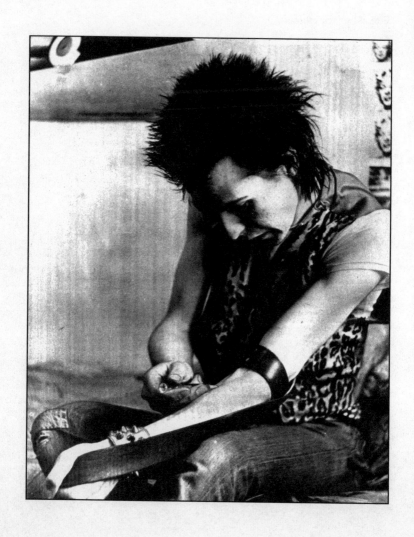

Sid Vicious

"You shall live, like Moses, you will prosper. And you, Ace, must die, because you have a brain the same size as me"
(from *Tuinals From Hell* by Legs McNeil)

There is a certain part of New York city that almost seems dirtier, somewhat sleazier than the rest. Most of it can be traced in a straight line from the club CBGB's to the hotel known as The Chelsea. Guitars hang in thrift shops, that, if they could talk, would tell a story of heroin-soaked owners, who kept them in a state of semi-permanent hock in order to keep their own appointment with a chinese rock. If it's a sad story you are looking for you came to the right neighbourhood. In a small flat at 63 Bank Street, belonging to a sometime stripper and allegedly full-time prostitute who answered to the name of Michelle Robinson, in an even smaller bedroom, the most distinguishing feature of which was a swastika T-shirt, long overdue a wash, thrown in the corner of the floor, lay the recently dead body of Michelle's new boyfriend, not a pimp this time but a fully fledged rockstar. Only if the truth were told, it had been a full twelve months since this kid had enjoyed much in the way of stardom.

A twenty-one year old Simon Beverley lay dead in bed, forever now trapped in the persona of Sid Vicious, a persona given to him by his best friend John Joseph Lydon, the artist formally known as Johnny Rotten, and in fact a persona just too big for his shoulders from the day he first started carrying it around. A twenty one year old street punk kid, skinny as hell, who just maybe didn't die in vain, because even today they sell Tshirts in his name from Camden Town to Downtown Manhattan; but in a better world shouldn't he just be turning forty-six...

Simon John Beverley was the only son of Anne Beverley (nee Randell) and John Ritchie. His mother a one time heroin addict and sometime cleaner at Ronnie Scotts Jazz Club in Soho, London, was his only stable parent. John Ritchie, a Scots guardsman and sometime guard at Buckingham Palace (although discharged long before 1977, making John Lydon's comments in the movie *Filth And The Fury* just plain silly!) stayed around long enough to promise Anne a taste of the good life with their new-born son, but then vanished into thin air; although to his credit – unlike Freddie Lennon and Tommy Gallagher, both before and after him – he didn't resurface once his son had tasted fame.

The childhood of the future Sex Pistol was nothing special, a brief spell on the hippy trail with his mother in Spain was followed by a return to the family bosom (Anne's mother and sister) in London, before Anne married Chris Beverley, a well spoken, well dressed, professional gentleman from a moneyed background. Just as it looked like Anne and her child had won the lottery, Chris Beverley died of cancer eight months after the wedding. His parents stepped in and sent young Simon to public school, but that didn't suit and very soon mother and son were back in Soho. The young Simon Beverley changed his fate at secondary school, the day, to be exact, that he met a skinny London-Irish kid named Lydon. The meeting of the two made sparks fly, and before long, via an ex-member of The Pink Floyd crossed with a toothless hamster, Simon Beverley was renamed Sid Vicious.

When Lydon later met and joined The Swankers, a group from the wrong end of Kings road, who fast became the Sex Pistols, Sid's job became that of court jester, chief hanger-on and super fan. He loved the Pistols more than he had ever worshipped Marc Bolan or David Bowie, and because his best mate was their lead singer he got to hold court with them, something he'd only been able to dream of with Bolan and Bowie. The group rocketed to fame via a few rude words on a live, primetime television show, and a seemingly revolving door-style record deal, which started life at EMI, called in at A&M for less than a week and tipped up at Virgin. Before EMI had seen the back of them however, the group sacked its bass player Glen Matlock, for the almost deadly crime of listening to The Beatles, or at least that's what their manager's official press statement had said. More likely Matlock, the only genuine musician among them, had seen the circus this group were fast becoming from too close up and jumped ship. His replacement, having never played a bass guitar in his life, but with a CV full to busting with the sort of image and attitude the group's manager was falling over himself to find – including having swung a bike chain at NME scribe Nick Kent at an earlier Pistols gig, plus the overriding fact that he may or may not have invented the pogo, the dance favoured by the high court of King Rotten – was Sid Vicious.

"Junk is the ultimate merchandise, and the customer will crawl through a sewer and beg to buy it"
(William Burroughs)

With his new found stardom came the permanent fixture in his life, that everyone else referred too as Nancy. A super groupie and ex-prostitute, who arrived in the UK on the coat tails of The Heartbreakers, decided punk rock was the life style for her and went out to snare herself a boyfriend. When she reached the door marked Sex Pistols, she first tried it on with Rotten, only to be passed on to guitarist Steve Jones, known to fuck anything with a pulse, who had his turn on the Nancy cycle and then moved her on to Sid. Our unfortunate hero got it all wrong and fell in love, but the love of a "good" woman never comes cheap, and Nancy was no exception, but she didn't want the jewels or a big house in the country, she wanted heroin and, before too long, so did our hero.

Fast becoming the inept idiot on bass in the eyes of his former best mate, Sid sank deeper into his lair in Pindock Mews (Maida Vale, London), deeper into heroin and deeper into Nancy's web. By January 1978, less than a year after Sid had become a Sex Pistol, they were on tour in the USA and fast becoming part of their own myth. On the 14th of that month at The Winterland Ballroom in San Francisco (in front of their biggest paying crowd to date, 5000 punters) the group fell apart. Rotten walked away with a sneer to the bosom of Warner Brothers Records (their USA label), Jones and Paul Cook ran off to Brazil to take tea with a Great Train Robber and work on a movie, while Sid arrived back in England via a drugs overdose, with a plan of solo super stardom.

His first wrong move was telling the world that his new manager was his girlfriend, his second wrong move was actually looking up to Johnny Thunders and Dee Dee Ramone. With a plan so vague that even viewed from almost 25 years later it still seems silly, Sid and Nancy assembled a one-off group called The Vicious White Kids, featuring; Glen Matlock (bass guitar), Steve New (lead guitar) and Rat Scabies (drums). They played only one gig at The Electric Ballroom in London's trendy Camden Town, took the proceeds to buy flight tickets and moved to New York. Their plan seemed simple on paper – Sid would be a star in New York City. Unfortunately, in the New York at which they arrived, even the Sex Pistols didn't even mean that much, so Sid Vicious on his own was a non-starter. With no recording deal, only a handful of small club gigs to their joint name, and a bunch of friends you would be happy to call enemies, they bedded in at The Chelsea Hotel, a hang-out for drug-addicted low-life since time began. It was at The Chelsea in the early hours of October 13th 1978 (a little over three months after they arrived) that Sid awoke from a drug induced semi-coma, to find a trail of blood from the bed to the bathroom. Under the sink Nancy Laura

Spungen lay dead; she was twenty years old. Sid in a state of shock rang for an ambulance, but was greeted by the police. According to *The New York Post* later that day, Sid Vicious was seized at Chelsea Hotel, and accused of slaying his girlfriend. If he'd come to New York looking for a moment in the spotlight he'd certainly found it; by the time the story hit the evening news both his mother and former Pistols manager Malcolm McLaren were in New York. One sold stories to the newspapers, the other tried to cut a recording deal, but the Sid that finally emerged from Rikers Island Prison on twenty-five thousand dollars bail (posted by Virgin Records) was a washed-up shadow of his former self, having been beaten and raped by genuine street punks. He mumbled his way through a few interviews, attempted suicide by slashing his arms open with a broken light bulb, got himself a new (equally screwed up) girlfriend in the shape of Michelle Robinson, and found himself back in Rikers Island after attacking Todd Smith (brother of Patti) in Hurrah's nightclub. The game, in effect, was all but over.

A trial date was set for February 1st 1979, for which Malcolm talked Virgin into standing bail once again, if this time Sid would record an album of standards backed by Steve Jones and Paul Cook. All was looking very well with the plan, the remaining Pistols and McLaren were due to fly out to New York on February 3rd. Even a betting man would have called good odds on witness statements still being taken by then, but that was without counting on the genius of F. Lee Bailey (who years later would pull similar rabbits out of the same hat for OJ Simpson) who had been hired by Virgin to represent Sid. The trial started at lunch time and little before five that afternoon Sid was once again walking free on bail. He walked straight into the waiting arms of his mother (a women barely capable of looking after herself), Michelle Robinson, photographer Eileen Polk and fellow drug addict Eliot Kidd. A release party was planned at Michelle's flat in Bank Street. Sid's favourite beer was already waiting,

straight to hell

spaghetti bolognaise was cooked in his honour. Unfortunately (thanks to Mum) heroin was also laid on, in what would later turn out to be the purest street form Manhattan had seen in years (98% pure smack). Sid took some of the drug at the party, turned blue, almost overdosed, took another beer and carried on chatting. According to those present all the talk that night was positive, he could beat this rap, his album could go platinum without fail. But at sometime during the night (even those present don't know exactly when) Sid took the rest of the heroin from his mother's purse and fell into the deepest sleep of all. He was twenty-one years old. In his favour we must remember he was facing 27 years to life, in a prison were he had already been beaten and raped, and was mortally wounded by grief for his dead Nancy, so what would you have done... Later, an apparent suicide note was found stuffed inside Sid's passport.

we had a death pact
i have to keep my half of the
bargain.
please bury me next to my baby.
bury me in my leather jacket
and motor cycle boots.
goodbye

KILLING FOR CULTURE
David Kerekes & David Slater

AN ILLUSTRATED HISTORY OF DEATH FILM

KILLING FOR CULTURE is a definitive investigation into the urban myth of the "snuff movie". Includes: Feature Film, Mondo Film, and Death Film – from *Faces Of Death* to real deaths captured on film such as live-TV suicides, executions, and news footage. Illustrated by stunning photographs from cinema, documentary and real life, KILLING FOR CULTURE is a necessary book which examines and questions the human obsession with images of violence, dismemberment and death, and the way our society is coping with an increased profusion of these disturbing yet compelling images from all quarters. Includes a complete filmography and index.

"Well-researched and highly readable, Killing For Culture *is a must-have."* –Film Threat

www.creationbooks.com

www.creationbooks.com